167820

Garten, Hugh Fred-
erick

Wagner the drama-
tist

DATE DUE

WAGNER THE DRAMATIST

An engraving of Richard Wagner.

WAGNER
THE DRAMATIST

by
H. F. Garten

Wagners Dichtertum anzuzweifeln scheint mir immer absurd.
Thomas Mann

ROWMAN AND LITTLEFIELD
TOTOWA, NEW JERSEY

First published in the United States 1978
by Rowman and Littlefield, Totowa, N.J.

ISBN 0-8476-6058-3

Originally published in Great Britain 1977 by
John Calder (Publishers) Ltd.

167820

Printed and Bound in Scotland

CONTENTS

Introduction   7

I   Apprenticeship   15

II   The Romantic Outsider:
        Der fliegende Holländer   31
        Tannhäuser   37
        Lohengrin   53

III   From History to Myth   60

IV   The Theory of Drama   71

V   World Myth: *Der Ring des Nibelungen*   80

VI   Love and Death: *Tristan und Isolde*   104

VII   Mastership: *Die Meistersinger von Nürnberg*   115

VIII Satirical Interlude   132

IX   The Myth of Redemption: *Parsifal*   135

Bibliography   151

Index   157

Page

"Rienzi in the Forum," painting by Alfred
Elmore, 1844.   27

Der fliegende Holländer, London production, 1876.   33

Tannhäuser, miniature from the *Manessische
Handschrift,* 13th century.   45

Tannhäuser, the first production, Dresden, 1845.   49

Lohengrin: departure of the swan knight.   58

Das Rheingold: Alberich and the Rhine maidens.   83

Die Walküre: the death of Siegmund.   88

Siegfried: Brünnhilde's awakening.   91

Götterdämmerung: the dead Siegfried.   101

Tristan und Isolde: woodcuts, Augsburg, 1484.   110

Nuremberg at the time of Hans Sachs.   118

Hans Sachs, woodcut by Michael Ostendorfer, 1545.   118

Die Meistersinger: Eva and Hans Sachs.   126

The apparition of the Holy Grail, from a 15th
century manuscript of the *Conte del Graal.*   139

Kundry leads Parsifal to the Grail Castle.   146

Acknowledgements

I should like to thank Mr. Andrew Medlicott for providing
most of the illustrations, also Mr. V. J. Riley and the staff
of the Institute of Germanic Studies, University of London,
the librarians of the Goethe-Institut, London, and of the
Bibliothèque Nationale, Paris. Above all, I am indebted to
Dr. Kurt Mitchells for his advice and help.

A.G.

I

INTRODUCTION

Richard Wagner's dual genius as musician and dramatist is unique in the history of the arts. Of course there were opera composers before him (e.g. Lortzing) who provided their own libretti, but simply as vehicles for the music, without literary pretensions. Wagner's "libretti", however, are poetic creations in their own right. No matter whether they are considered better or worse than other libretti, they are of an altogether different order, conceived by the same creative imagination as the music. In their many-levelled complexity and their symbolic significance they answer to the highest claims of drama in its classical sense. Wagner's characters— Tristan, Isolde, Marke, Siegmund, Siegfried, Wotan, Brünn-hilde, Hans Sachs, Kundry—are as alive and unique as those of any great dramatist. And they are so not only by force of the music, like other operatic characters: they have an additional dimension as dramatic creations in the full sense of the word. The term "libretti" seems thus quite inappropriate to Wagner's texts. Wagner himself called them *Dichtung* and claimed for himself the rank of a *Dichter*, a poet. His vast literary oeuvre, especially his chief theoretical work, *Opera and Drama*, deals almost as much with poetic as with musical issues. He placed Shakespeare next to Beethoven and by implication saw himself as a fusion of the two.

Wagner's achievements as a dramatist have been neglected for obvious reasons: musicologists are not interested in them, and literary critics do not take them seriously since he was after all merely a composer of operas. Medievalists, on the other hand, scorn him for "corrupting" the genuine epics on which his works are largely based. Of course most of the countless books on Wagner also include an appraisal of his texts. There are even some which concentrate on the dramatic and textual aspects. But they are often blurred by a specific ideological angle which singles out one aspect at the expense of others (such as Shaw's Marxist interpretation in *The Perfect Wagnerite*). It is therefore tempting to trace Wagner's evolution purely as a dramatist—always bearing in mind that one dimension of his work, the music, is deliberately excluded. This approach will have the advantage of including the numerous works which never reached completion—drafts and scenarios which he abandoned or which were not intended to be set to music. Of course it is impossible not to touch occasionally on the music. For Wagner's texts are written for music; they would hardly have survived without it. Any attempts to stage them as straight plays (and such attempts have been made) are bound to fail. Even *Die Meistersinger,* undoubtedly his most accomplished work in literary terms, would pose insuperable problems as its very subject is the art of song.

The coordination of text and music in Wagner's mind will always remain a mystery. For all his voluminous self-interpretations and theorisings, he has never revealed the secret of his creative process. To what extent did he have the music in mind when writing the text? His manuscripts bear no indications except a few occasional scribbles on the margin—for the most part merely rhythmical patterns, hardly ever even a short tune. In some instances many years separated the conception of the drama and the start of composition: between the first detailed draft of *Die Meistersinger* and its composition seventeen years elapsed, between the first sketch of *Parsifal* and its composition twelve years. It is scarcely conceivable that all that time the music should have been in his mind. True, he usually started on the music soon after completing the full text. But there are many indications in his letters that the actual musical inspiration occurred only after the text was completed. In short, the way Wagner's creative mind actually worked remains impenetrable.

All the more time and effort did he expend on discussing

theoretically the interrelation of drama and music—the basic problem of opera from the beginning of its history. No other composer has produced a comparable volume of theoretical writings, expounding his artistic aims and interpreting his own works. His literary works alone, not including his vast correspondence, comprise 16 volumes in the German edition—sufficient for the life-work of any writer. These writings accompanied his creative work throughout his life, propagating his revolutionary ideas about the *Gesamt-kunstwerk*, the total work of art he was aiming at, and ranging over the whole field of art and its relation to society. This combination of subconscious creativity and intellectual consciousness, of intuition and reflection, makes Wagner a towering figure not only in the history of music but also in the history of ideas. "Let us not underrate the power of reflection," Wagner once wrote; "the work of art produced unconsciously belongs to periods far removed from ours: the work of art of the highest period of intellectual culture *(Bildungsperiode)* can be produced only in full consciousness."

Of course Wagner's theories of the arts and their evolution through the ages must not be taken as objective histori-ography. They are intensely subjective and converge on one single point: his own work, that is, the fusion of drama and music. The principles of this fusion and the history of its two components are the subject of Wagner's major theoretical treatise, *Opera and Drama*, of 1851, as well as of numerous essays written before and after. His ideas have been amply discussed in the vast literature on Wagner; they will be outlined in the course of this study only in so far as they are relevant to the dramatic aspect of his work. The central proposition, namely, that in the "work of art of the future" *drama* must be the *end, music* the *means* of expression, seems to give pride of place to the text, assigning to music merely the role of illustrating and interpreting the verbal drama. (Wagner rejected to the very last the term "music drama" and insisted on calling his works "dramas"). This was indeed his thesis at the height of his fight against conventional opera, that is, in the long creative pause between *Lohengrin* and the *Ring*, when he was trying to clear the ground before setting out on his new road. This thesis has, however, been open to misunderstanding: his concept of "drama" does not in fact apply to verbal drama only. It includes the music as a "means of expression"—and not only the music but also gesture, decor, and all other components of stage representation. In short, "drama" is "the total work of art".

In his later years, however, a slight shift of emphasis may be discerned. It was mainly under the impact of Schopenhauer that Wagner began to assign to music the primary place among the arts. He defined drama as *ersichtlich gewordene Taten der Musik* (deeds or acts of music made visible) and, in connection with *Tristan,* spoke of *die Kunst des tönenden Schweigens* (the art of sounding silence). In fact, *Tristan* is the work in which the music is most self-contained, in other words, in which the words are most subordinate to the music. Nevertheless, even in this extreme instance, the music is determined by the drama. It is never "absolute", that is, following its own immanent laws; it is always determined by extra-musical factors, whether language, gesture, scenic action, character, or even abstract concepts.

All this must be kept in mind if we single out one main component of Wagner's *Gesamtkunstwerk,* namely, the verbal drama as presented in the text. Nothing is easier than to let oneself be carried along on the ebb and flow of the music, perhaps with some cursory knowledge of the "story". Unfortunately, this is what most non-German-speaking listeners are reduced to, and it speaks for the power of Wagner's music that it can be done. But any deeper understanding of these many-levelled works is possible only if one knows what it is all about—the web of ideas underlying the drama, the changes and modifications they have undergone during the time of germination. For each of these works—at any rate from *Tannhäuser* on—is the product of extensive studies of historical and literary sources, transformed and re-interpreted by the creative imagination.

It is a well known fact that Wagner was a late developer. At an age when most other composers had already achieved some masterpieces or at any rate established their unmistakable identity, Wagner was drifting aimlessly, unsure which way to go. What is more, for quite some time he vacillated between drama and music: Shakespeare was to him no less a guiding star than Beethoven. In short, Wagner's beginnings had definitely something dilettantish about them. He openly acknowledged this later. In 1862, looking back on his youth, he wrote, "I remember still asking myself doubtingly around my thirtieth year whether I really had the makings of a supreme artistic individuality: I could still sense in my work influence and imitation, and only with anxiety dared look upon my further development as an original creator." Outwardly he was the typical provincial conductor, eager to gain local success through some composition of his own. Up to the age of 28, his works were in no way above the general run and indeed showed little originality: *Die Feen*—a romantic fairy-tale opera in the style of Weber and Marschner, followed by its diametrical opposite, *Das Liebesverbot,* a comic opera in the Italian-French style of Donizetti and Auber; then *Rienzi*—a spectacular grand opera trying to outstrip Meyerbeer. But these diverse works had one thing in common: the texts, though little more than conventional libretti drawn from any convenient source, were written by Wagner himself. From the very start it would never have occurred to him to set someone else's text to music; instead, he was to provide, as we shall see, texts for other composers. None of all these works gave the slightest hint of things to come; they were rather the products of a moderately talented young composer eager to make his name in one way or another.

The breakthrough came in 1841 with *Der fliegende Holländer*—curiously enough, when he was down-and-out in Paris. In his autobiography, *My Life,* Wagner describes in detail how it was precisely his frustration in the French capital that roused in him a longing for Germany and the world of medieval legend. Only from then on, he writes, did he become a *Dichter*; from then on, every work is unmistakably his own, flesh of his flesh; the central characters—the Dutchman, Tannhäuser, Lohengrin, Tristan, Hans Sachs—embodying successive stages of his autobiography. Wagner's whole life-work is really one single work evolving step by step with logical consistency; each work contains the germs of the next. Between the ages of 32 and 36, the seeds were laid for virtually all the future works down to what he knew would be his last, *Parsifal*. Here, too, we find the peculiar combination of conscious planning and unconscious creativity.

All Wagner's texts (with the exception of *Die Meistersinger*) are derived from epic sources. It was his particular genius to transform narrative into dramatic art, condensing a long line of episodes into three pregnant situations and reducing a vast array of characters to a small number of archetypal figures. However, in this dramatic compression the works still have epic dimensions. Everything is on a superhuman scale; the characters are over-lifesize. All external action is reduced to a few climactic moments, whereas the inner drama, unfolding in dialogue and monologue, proceeds at a slow pace. In this respect, Wagner's dramatic structures show affinity to those of Ibsen, who uses the same technique of condensing a complex sequence of events into a few symbolic situations played out between two or three characters.

Wagner's model was of course Greek drama. In his accounts of his adolescent years, his discovery of the Greek tragedians and the impact they had on him play an important part. And his various writings about the origin of drama take their point of departure from the Athenian stage as the supreme form of theatre, carried by the *Volk*, the people.* The whole history of the theatre is presented as a decline from that height—with the exception of Shakespeare, whose drama was also an expression of the *Volk*. By implication (and sometimes explicitly) Wagner sees his own work as an attempt to renew the art of drama out of the *Volksgeist*, the spirit of the people. This is the impulse that drove him to the legends and romances of the Middle Ages and further back to

---

* The German word *Volk*—a key-term in Wagner's aesthetics—is only inadequately rendered by the English "people", which lacks its mystique, deeply rooted in German Romantic thought. Nor will the English "folk" do, though some of its original force is still retained in such words as "folksong" and "folklore". I shall therefore use throughout Wagner's term *Volk* and its compounds *Volksgeist, Volksepos,* etc.

the Nordic myths of the *Edda* whose roots are lost in prehistoric times. For the true creator of these myths was the *Volk*, and Wagner, renewing them in the light of his own times, was its mouthpiece.

This, at any rate, is how he saw himself and wanted to be seen. To what extent he actually believed in this claim is difficult to judge. He always was a past master in underpinning his creative work with theoretical arguments. The theatre he finally built at Bayreuth had little in common (except in the shape of the auditorium) with the theatre of ancient Athens. It was not so much a theatre of the *Volk* as one built to serve a single purpose—the performance of Wagner's work. And yet there was some truth in his recourse to the *Volk*: his work was written consciously against his own age, against a civilisation which he abhorred and which he saw represented by the court theatres of Germany and the Grand Opéra of Paris with their superficial entertainment for a leisured class. The political revolutionary and the opera reformer were one and the same: Wagner's youthful rebellion against a sterile social order and his fight against outworn operatic conventions sprang from the same source. The astonishing thing is that the political rebel and outcast in the end turned into the established master, a national figurehead—Hans Sachs hailed by the *Volk*. So at any rate in the field of art he achieved his aim. And art was after all what really mattered to him, as Hans Sachs confirms with his closing words.

I have refrained from citing, either approvingly or critically, any of the secondary literature on Wagner. Instead, I have preferred to let him speak himself wherever it seemed relevant to the subject. Probably no other creative artist has commented so lavishly on his own works and artistic aims. Not that these comments can always be taken at face value. His intense egocentricity, his almost obsessive urge for self-explanation and self-interpretation, colour his autobiographical and theoretical writings as well as his vast correspondence. But these writings are invaluable for shedding light on the genesis of the works and the various stages they passed through. There are three main autobiographical writings: the *Autobiographische Skizze (Autobiographical Sketch)* which covers his early years up to his return from Paris in 1842, *Eine Mitteilung an meine Freunde (A Communication to my Friends)*, which gives a detailed account of his artistic development up to 1851, the beginning of his exile, and, finally, his principal autobiographical work, *Mein Leben (My Life)*, which ends with the miraculous turn of his fortunes, the invitation of King Ludwig II of Bavaria in 1864. For the last twenty years, which saw the completion of *Die Meistersinger* and the *Ring* and the composition of *Parsifal*, we have no detailed documentation apart from private letters and essays on specific subjects.

I

APPRENTICESHIP

In the opening pages of his autobiography *My Life,* Wagner traces in detail the artistic influences of his early youth. What is most striking at first sight is the fact that he places poetic and theatrical impressions before musical ones. Through his stepfather, Ludwig Geyer, an actor and playwright, he was introduced to the world of the theatre which from the very first held him in its spell. What attracted him was (as he puts it) "not so much the wish for entertainment and diversion as the contact with an element which, in contrast to the impressions of everyday life, represented an utterly different, purely phantastic world . . ." (XIII,17)

At the Dresden Kreuzschule, which he attended from his tenth to his fifteenth year, his dominant interests were Greek mythology, legend, and ancient history. One of his teachers encouraged him to try his hand at an epic poem, *The Battle of Parnassos,* and a tragedy on *The Death of Odysseus,* neither of which got very far. "I wanted to become a poet," he writes in his *Autobiographical Sketch.* "I drafted tragedies on the model of the Greeks." (I, 5). He even claims to have translated twelve cantos from Homer's *Odyssey* when he was twelve years old.

His greatest admiration, however, was reserved for Shakespeare. "Once I even learnt English and this only to get to know Shakespeare exactly. I translated metrically Romeo's monologue. I soon dropped English again, but Shakespeare remained my model." (I, 5). It was under the impact of Shakespeare that he embarked at the age of thirteen on a full-length tragedy, *Leubald und Adelaide,* which occupied him for two years. It was, as he recalls, an amalgam of *Hamlet, Macbeth,* and *Lear,* in the course of which no less than 42 characters died a violent death. In the end he was compelled to let some of them reappear as ghosts since he would otherwise have run out of characters in the last act. In his autobiography Wagner gives a fairly detailed account of the plot which, he admits, was a variation on *Hamlet,* the main difference being that the ghost of the hero's father (killed under similar circumstances) orders his son to avenge his death on the entire clan of his enemies.

Of this tragedy only a few pages survive, containing a scene at a hermitage written in blank verse. This small sample is enough to show that this juvenile work in no way surpasses the general run of adolescent literary efforts. There is, however, one point of interest: Wagner concludes his account with the words: "I knew what nobody could yet know, namely, that my work could only be properly judged when it was provided with the music I had resolved to write for it." (XIII, 36). That music was never written. However, the intention shows that already at that early stage Wagner conceived music as a means of heightening the effect of drama.

The kind of music he had in mind was Beethoven's incidental music to Goethe's *Egmont,* that is, not full-scale opera but melodrama, with overture, interludes and intermittent songs. In short, the drama was to be the dominant factor. In order to acquire the necessary musical technique, he borrowed a manual *Method of Thorough-Bass* from a lending library. When this proved insufficient, he secretly took lessons from a member of the Leipzig orchestra. These instructions, however, filled him with "great repugnance"; music was to him a demonic element, "a mystical, sublime monstrosity; any rules seemed to me to distort it." (XIII, 43). Much more to his taste were the tales of E. T. A. Hoffmann, whom he calls his "favourite author". His mind was steeped in the phantastic world of that writer, above all the demonic figure of Kapellmeister Kreisler. It is not surprising that he found in Hoffmann, with his blend of literary and musical elements, a kindred spirit to whom he returned more than once for inspiration.

At the same time, Wagner's involvement in the theatre received a fresh impulse; what in his childhood years had been merely "a phantastic curiosity" now grew into "a more thorough, more conscious passion". Through his sister Rosalie, who had become a member of the Leipzig theatre company, he had free access to the performances; he saw in quick succession *Julius Caesar*, *Macbeth*, *Hamlet*, the plays of Schiller, and Goethe's *Faust*, along with the operas of Weber and Marschner. But all these impressions were surpassed by a performance of *Fidelio*, with the great dramatic singer Wilhelmine Schröder-Devrient in the title role. This "miracle" (as he calls it in his memoirs) "suddenly gave my artistic feelings a new direction, decisive for my whole life . . . Looking back, I can hardly find any event that had so profound an effect upon me". (XIII, 50).

The "new direction" was no doubt the realisation that the fulfilment of his artistic ambitions was a synthesis of drama and music, in short, opera. From then on, music entered his life as an equal partner to literature, and Beethoven became, next to Shakespeare, a cornerstone of his imaginative world. In his mind, the two merged into one: "In my ecstatic dreams, I encountered both, saw them and talked to them . . ." (XIII, 41). Shakespeare and Beethoven—these two were to remain his supreme idols throughout his life.

Wagner's first attempt at opera was *Die Hochzeit (The Wedding)*, the text of which he wrote during a stay in Prague in 1832, when he was nineteen. Of this text only the opening scene has survived. But in his autobiography he gives a comprehensive summary of the action, describing it as a "complete night-piece of the blackest hue." (XIII, 93). The plot echoes to some extent his juvenile drama *Leubald und Adelaide*. Once again there are two families locked in deadly feud. In an attempt at reconciliation the head of one of the houses has invited his enemy's son to the wedding of his daughter Ada. Unfortunately the young man falls in love with the bride at first sight. Driven by his dark passion he climbs up to the balcony of the bridal chamber where Ada is waiting for the bridegroom. In defence of her honour she hurls the intruder over the balustrade into the courtyard where he is found dead by his companions. Suspecting their hosts of foul play, they swear vengeance. The bride's father, to prevent a renewal of the feud, promises to have the murdered man buried in the presence of his whole clan; a divine sign will reveal who is guilty. Meanwhile the bride shows signs of growing madness; she evades the bridegroom and locks herself in her room. However, at the funeral she appears at the head of her women, and as the body is carried past sinks lifeless to the ground; the culprit is revealed and the two families stand in silent awe.

It would not be difficult to discover here hints of later works and dramatic situations, such as the bridal chamber in *Lohengrin* or Hagen at the bier of Siegfried. However—as far as can be judged from the remaining fragment—the treatment was still immature, in the style of the romantic drama of fate much in vogue at the time. As for the music, it is doubtful whether much more was written than a septet for the opening scene.

A few months later, in the winter of 1832, Wagner embarked on what was to be his first completed opera, *Die Feen (The Fairies)*. The subject was taken from a play by the 18th century Venetian Carlo Gozzi, *La donna serpente*, but he transferred the scene from a fairy-tale Orient to an imaginary medieval Germany, giving the characters such Teutonic names as Morald, Gunther, and Gernot. The two principal characters, the fairy Ada and prince Arindal, bear the same names as those in *Die Hochzeit*. In every other respect, the two works are diametrically opposed. While *Die Hochzeit*, according to Wagner's own description, dispenses with any operatic adornments, *Die Feen* uses every conventional device of opera: there are three couples of lovers, one idealised, one realistic, one coarse and comic. As for the poetic diction, Wagner proceeded, as he himself admits, "with an almost deliberate carelessness." (XIII, 99). In short, he had for the time being discarded all literary ambitions; he was simply a composer who wanted to provide himself with a suitable opera text. This, then, is the plot of

Die Feen: Prince Arindal has been living for seven years in fairy-land with the fairy Ada who is deeply in love with him. One day his former companions find him there and inform him that his country is in grave danger. Ada herself persuades him to go back as she is forced by a decree of the fairy king to subject her lover to a severe test before she is allowed to join him as a mortal. Maddened by various ordeals, Arindal is led to believe that Ada is an evil sorceress, and curses her. Whereupon Ada, despairing of his love, reveals to him that she is now condemned to be turned into stone. (In Gozzi's play she is transformed into a serpent whom the prince redeems with a kiss). In the last act Arindal realises that she was all along innocent and fights his way to a subterranean grotto where Ada is turned to stone. With his song of love and remorse he frees her from the spell, and the fairy-world opens up to admit them both to a life of eternal bliss.*

It would be easy to trace parallels between this somewhat muddled plot and Tannhäuser in the Venusberg; there is even a foretaste of *Lohengrin*: early on the prince temporarily forfeits the love of the fairy by asking her name! However, the action lacks any genuine dramatic conflict: "good" and "evil" are hopelessly entangled and all the hero's ordeals turn out to be mere delusions, manipulated by the fairies themselves.

Wagner spent the next year, 1833, setting the text to music in what he calls "the German style", that is, in the vein of Weber and Marschner. He even conducted some fragments from it in a concert performance. But his attempts to have the whole work produced at Nuremberg or Leipzig, where he had close personal connections, proved in vain. *Die Feen* was

---

* It is not known whether Hofmannsthal, when writing the text for *Die Frau ohne Schatten (The Woman without a Shadow)* was familiar with Wagner's first opera. There are certainly some striking parallels: the interplay of the fairy and the human worlds, the Emperor's transformation into stone, only to be redeemed by his repentant wife, and other similarities. However, these may well be recurrent motives of romantic fairy-tale rather than conscious borrowings.

not published and performed until 1888, five years after Wagner's death.

It is difficult to imagine a great contrast than that between *Die Feen* and Wagner's next work, *Das Liebesverbot (The Ban on Love)*. If the former was steeped in the spirit of German romanticism, the latter was consciously conceived as a comic opera in the Italian style. Several factors combined to cause this radical change. One was the impact made on Wagner's receptive mind by a performance of Bellini's opera *I Capuletti ed i Montecchi* (once again with Schröder-Devrient in the part of Romeo). It caused him to ponder how such "shallow and empty music" could make so deep an impression compared with the ineffectiveness of "solid German music" as applied to opera. Without delving too deeply into the problem, he followed, as he writes, "rudderless the stream of my excited youthful emotions", (XIII, 110) turning away from the seriousness which had up to then led him to romantic mysticism. The immediate reflection of this change of taste can be seen in an essay written the following year, 1834, entitled *Die deutsche Oper (The German Opera)*—the first in a long line of theoretical writings. In this striking essay he contends that the true domain of German music was instrumental music, while there was no such thing as a German opera. "We are too intellectual and far too learned to create warm human characters." Mozart could do so only through the beauty of Italian song. He goes on to extol Bellini's opera in which, after having tired of "the eternally allegorising orchestral bustle" he could at last enjoy simple, noble song (XII, 2).

These arguments are all the more striking in view of the road Wagner was to take later on. They illustrate the lack of conscious direction at this early stage in his development. The second contributory factor was of a more general nature. In the early 1830s, a new literary movement had emerged in the wake of the Paris July revolution. Although that revolution had comparatively few political repercussions in Germany (unlike the 1848 revolution which held such far-reaching consequences for Wagner's life), it left deep traces in the literary field. The new movement known as Young

Germany was led by such writers as Heine, Laube and Gutzkow. Wagner, then in his eighteenth year, had taken an active part in a student rising in Leipzig (a foretaste of his revolutionary sympathies eighteen years later). Shortly after, he had made friends with Laube, who had even offered him a libretto on the Polish national hero Kosziuszko. In 1833, Laube's novel *Das junge Europa (Young Europe)* began to appear, promulgating the political, moral and aesthetic ideals of the movement. These ideals were directed in the first place against the mysticism and political conservatism of the Romantics, pitting a realistic, materialistic world-view against their faded idealism, and propagating "free love" and the "emancipation of the flesh".

How eagerly the young Wagner embraced these ideas is vividly described in his *Autobiographical Sketch* of 1842: "At that time I was twenty-one years old, inclined to *joie de vivre* and a joyous view of the world . . . I had emerged from abstract mysticism and I learned to love material things. Beauty of matter, wit, and esprit were glorious things to me . . . Everything around me appeared to me as if in a ferment, and abandoning myself to this ferment seemed to me the most natural thing." (I, 10). He devoured Heine, Laube, and Heinse's 18th century novel *Ardinghello,* which preached the gospel of pagan sensuality.

It was under the influence of these ideas that Wagner turned to Shakespeare's *Measure for Measure* for his comic opera *Das Liebesverbot* or *Die Novize von Palermo (The Ban on Love* or *The Novice of Palermo).* However, he completely changed the serious substance of the play to remodel it "in the light of Young Europe", making free and unfettered sensuality triumph over puritan hypocrisy. With this aim in mind, he transferred the scene from Shakespeare's Vienna to 16th century Sicily. More important, he completely eliminated the figure of the Duke. The part of Angelo is taken by Friedrich, a German, acting as deputy for the absent king. It is this Friedrich who tries to suppress the carefree gaiety of the hot-blooded populace by proscribing the Carnival with all its attendant licentiousness. From the outset Wagner expands the scope of the action by including a large number of minor characters, with "the people" taking a major part in the proceedings. His version opens on a tumultuous scene of Friedrich's henchmen smashing up popular places of entertainment while the crowd tries in vain to stop them. The main action roughly follows Shakespeare's play, reducing its five acts to two. Claudio, a nobleman, has been arrested and sentenced to death for seducing a girl. His friend Luzio urges Claudio's sister Isabella, a novice in a convent, to throw herself at Friedrich's feet and plead for her brother's life. Friedrich is inflamed by Isabella's beauty and promises to pardon her brother on condition that she gives herself to him. In Wagner's version, it is Isabella who hits upon the idea of substituting Friedrich's abandoned wife, Mariana, for herself. She sends word to Friedrich to meet her under cover of the Carnival, which the people prepare to celebrate in defiance of his decree. Friedrich (like another Scarpia) has secretly given orders to have Claudio executed despite his promise, but Isabella intercepts his dispatch and, discovering the deceit, appeals to the people. Friedrich and Mariana are unmasked; the culprit stands revealed. "Sentence me by my own law!" he demands, to which the people defiantly reply that the law is abolished. Claudio is led in triumph from prison, Isabella, instead of returning to the convent, accepts Luzio, who has all the time been in love with her, and all form up in a joyful procession to meet the returning king.

It is clear from this brief summary that Wagner deliberately ignored the basic theme of Shakespeare's play, transforming it to a glorification of "free sensuality" as opposed to puritan repression. He himself sums up the essential difference: "Shakespeare solves the conflicts through the public return of the Duke, who has all along acted as an observer: his verdict is a serious one, based on the 'measure for measure' of the judge. I, however, cut the knot without the Duke by a revolution." (IV, 254). In pursuing his main purpose of providing himself with a text in the style of Italian comic opera, Wagner showed considerable skill. The action flows swiftly, divided in arias, duets, trios, choruses, and all the stock devices of the genre. "I proceeded with regard to diction and verse with far greater care than when I produced the text of *Die Feen,* just as I proceeded with the characterisation and partial invention of the situations with incomparably greater consciousness than had been the case in that earlier work." (XIII, 124).

Wagner spent the next year, with several interruptions, in setting his text to music. It was a crucial year both in his private and professional life: he met Minna Planer, his future wife, and he obtained his first appointment as musical director at Magdeburg. It was this position which gave him the chance of having his work staged. There were to be two performances at the end of the season, but owing to the near-bankruptcy of the management the season was shortened to end at Easter (1836), and only ten days were left for rehearsals. As during Lent no "frivolous" plays were permitted, there was a serious risk of the performance being prohibited. However, when Wagner assured the authorities that his work was based on a "serious play by Shakespeare", they contented themselves with a change of title; so the opera was staged under its subtitle, *Die Novize von Palermo.* Wagner gives an amusing account of that first performance. The première itself made no impression whatever, mainly, he maintains, owing to the insufficient rehearsal time and the lack of printed texts, which left the audience all but ignorant of the proceedings. For the second performance (which was to be for the benefit of the composer) only his landlady and a few others turned up. However, before the curtain rose a fight broke out backstage between the jealous husband of the primadonna and the second tenor. Since all participants, including the lady, were incapacitated, the producer was sent in front of the curtain to announce that owing to "unforeseen obstacles" the performance could not take place.

This, then, was the first public staging of a Wagner opera.*

Seen in the context of Wagner's whole work, *Das Liebesverbot* certainly seems an aberration: both textually and musically it was of no consequence for his further develop-

---

* Wagner presented the score of *Das Liebesverbot* to King Ludwig of Bavaria in 1866 with a dedicatory verse in which he called it "a sin of youth". It was not performed again until 1923.

ment. The contrast between it and its predecessor, *Die Feen,* suggests, however, that he had in him, as he puts it, "the capacity for developing in two fundamentally different directions." The harmonising of these two was to be, he concludes, "the work of my further artistic development." (IV, 255-6). In other words: the antithesis of sensuality and spirituality, separated in two contrasting works, subsequently formed the basic dramatic conflict within a single work.

It was to take many years before Wagner reached that stage. For the time being, he was overwhelmed by financial worries and driven by one urge only—to fight his way out of the misery of his external circumstances. After a vain attempt to have *Das Liebesverbot* performed at a Berlin theatre, Wagner took up a post as musical director in Königsberg (where he married Minna). In the autumn of 1837, he went to Riga where he spent the next two years. Although his professional duties left him little time for creative work, he explored a wide variety of books in search of operatic subjects. "Everything I read was of interest to me only according to its suitability as a subject for opera." (IV, 256).

After the failure of *Das Liebesverbot* he decided to produce a small-scale work adapted to the limited resources of provincial theatres. He found a suitable subject in a humorous tale from the *Arabian Nights,* which he transferred to contemporary Germany under the title *Männerlist grösser als Frauenlist oder Die glückliche Bärenfamilie (Man's Cunning Greater than Woman's or The Happy Bear Family).* As a matter of fact this is the only work of Wagner's set in modern times. The plot is pure farce: a wealthy jeweller has for reasons of his own hung a notice over his shop window bearing the inscription "Man's cunning greater than Woman's." A young lady, Leontine, stung by this notice, decides to play him a trick. She enters the shop heavily veiled and confides to the jeweller that she is the daughter of a nobleman who keeps her locked up, telling her would-be suitors that she is monstrously ugly—presumably to save the dowry. When she unveils, the jeweller is surprised by her beauty and resolves to marry her. He calls on her father—a conceited nobleman called the Baron of Eveningdew—and asks for her hand. After the marriage contract is drawn up the daughter is called in— and really turns out to be of forbidding ugliness. Leontine then reveals herself as a cousin of the bride and promises to save the desperate suitor from the marriage on condition that he removes the offending notice. The jeweller is about to comply when a scene outside his shop attracts his attention: a bear dancing to his master's pipe. This spectacle gives him an idea: he asks the bear-keeper to come to the betrothal celebrations at the Baron's house. There a large company of the Baron's relatives are assembled (with names like Morningmist, Nightshade, Mother of Pearl, etc.). When the bear-keeper appears the bridegroom embraces him, informing the stunned assembly that this is his long-lost father, while the bear sheds his skin and turns out to be his brother who has taken this disguise to earn a living. Appalled at the bridegroom's family, the Baron is glad to tear up the marriage contract, and the jeweller is free to marry Leontine, who gladly acknowledges that "man's cunning is greater than woman's."

This ludicrous plot Wagner treated in the style of the German *Singspiel* with prose dialogue and intermittent musical numbers. It is, in fact, unique within his entire work in making use of prose dialogue. Trivial as the action is, it is neither better nor worse than the general run of popular comedies of the period. The ridicule of aristocratic conceit, the basic theme of the play, was a subject much favoured by the bourgeois audiences of the time. But Wagner's main object in choosing this subject was obviously to provide a piece of light entertainment suitable for small theatres. He even started to set some of the numbers to music. Then, however, he realised "with revulsion" that he was once again about to write music "à la Adam" (the popular French composer of light opera). "My deeper feelings were disconsolate at this discovery."(I, 12). So he put the work aside, and never looked at it again.

It was his last attempt to stoop to the lower reaches of contemporary public taste in his frantic efforts to get a foothold on the operatic stage. In the summer of 1837, when he was on the way to his new appointment in Riga, he came across the old *Volksbuch* of *Till Eulenspiegel*, which suggested to him the idea of a "genuinely German comic opera". This plan came to nothing. But many years later, when working on his *Der junge Siegfried*, he vividly recalled the figure of the popular German jester.

Already at that early date, Wagner had his eyes on Paris, in the hope of trying his luck in what was then the centre of the operatic world. With this aim in mind he hit upon a curious plan: a novel by one H. König, *Die hohe Braut (The Noble Bride)* provided him with a plot for a grand opera in the French style. For the time being, he merely wrote a detailed prose draft which he sent to the ubiquitous French playwright Scribe (who provided libretti for a whole galaxy of operatic composers, including Verdi, Meyerbeer, Donizetti, and many others), with the suggestion to turn it into a full-scale libretto and commission him for the music. It seems that Scribe never responded to this proposition. But six years later, after his return from Paris, Wagner himself used this draft for a libretto of his own, though for another composer.

Of all the projects of that period of Wagner's life, only one came to full fruition—*Rienzi*. He had read Bulwer Lytton's historical novel about the 14th century Roman tribune who wanted to restore the glory of ancient Rome, and conceived the plan of an opera in the grand style. A performance of Spontini's *Fernand Cortez* he had seen in Berlin opened his eyes to the possibilities of a large-scale operatic work—an impression that played a significant part in his conception of *Rienzi, der letzte der Tribunen (Rienzi, the Last of the Tribunes)*. In working out his plan he deliberately proceeded on such an extravagant scale as to forestall any possibility of having it produced at a provincial theatre: the work was to "build a bridge" to the large European opera houses—above all, to Paris! "Grand opera, with all its scenic and musical splendour, its effective musical mass-passions, served me as a model; and it was my artistic ambition not just to imitate it but to surpass its previous realisations with ruthless extravagance." (IV, 258).Moreover, *Rienzi* offered

Rienzi in the Forum, painting by Alfred Elmore, 1844.

Wagner for the first time a subject with which he could seriously identify. Its popular hero, with his lofty ideas of liberty, surrounded by corruption and intrigue, touched a kindred chord in him. Nevertheless, he saw the subject still in terms of grand opera, with its five acts, its five spectacular finales of massed choruses, processions, and battle music. This conventional approach guided him in working out the libretto: "I applied no greater care with regard to diction and verse than seemed necessary in order to produce a good, not trivial, *opera text.*" (IV, 259). It was not his purpose, he asserts, to write duets and trios; but they occurred quite automatically in the course of writing; he even found a "natural" place for a ballet.

Within these limitations, the text of *Rienzi* shows considerable dramatic skill, surpassing the general level of contemporary opera libretti. The scene is set in 14th century Rome. The action opens with an abduction scene (reminiscent of Gilda's abduction in *Rigoletto,* written some twelve years later): Orsini, at the head of a group of nobles, puts a ladder against Rienzi's house to carry off Rienzi's sister Irene. They are disturbed by the Colonnas, another noble family. A fight which ensues between the two factions is interrupted by Adriano, Orsini's son, who frees Irene and takes her under his protection. Rienzi enters and upbraids the nobles for their lawless conduct, lamenting the decline of Rome from its former glory. He is acclaimed by the people who see in him their saviour from oppression and appoint him as their tribune. Adriano, though a nobleman, swears allegiance to Rienzi if he will give him Irene for his wife. The second act opens with a hymn of the 'Messengers of Peace', extolling Rome's newly gained freedom. Even the nobles pay homage to Rienzi, but secretly conspire to kill him and regain their power. Adriano, who has overheard them, is torn between his love for his father and his loyalty to Rienzi. During a festivity on the Capitol a mime is performed showing symbolically the rape of Lucretia by Tarquin and Rome's liberation from tyranny through Brutus. Recalling this early work in his *Communication to my Friends,* Wagner regrets that this mime was replaced by a conventional ballet which "distracted from my noble intentions and made this scene no more than an ordinary operatic feature." (IV, 259). At the end of this pageant Orsini rushes forward to kill Rienzi, but he is overpowered and sentenced to death. Rienzi, moved by Adriano's and Irene's pleas for mercy, pardons him. The nobles leave the city to collect an army and regain their power by force. As Rienzi goes out to meet them in battle, Adriano throws himself at his feet, imploring him to spare his father. Rienzi, disregarding his appeal, defeats the nobles and returns in triumph, while Orsini's body is brought in and Adriano swears to avenge his father's death.

In the fourth act, Rienzi's fortunes have changed: the German Emperor has turned against him, and the Church at the order of the Pope has sided with the nobles. As Rienzi approaches the Lateran church, he finds the doors closed against him. Deserted by his friends—at their head Adriano, now his sworn enemy—he retreats with Irene to the Capitol where he is besieged by the hostile populace. As the Capitol goes up in flames, Adriano tries to save Irene but perishes together with her and Rienzi. The final tableau foreshadows the close of *Götterdämmerung*:

> With a terrible crash, the Capitol collapses and buries Adriano too in its ruins . . .

This varied, highly dramatic action offered Wagner every conceivable device of grand opera in the style of Meyerbeer and Spontini—festive processions, battle hymns, monks' choruses, prayers, love duets, revenge arias, etc. But it also appealed, with its struggle between plebeians and patricians, and its popular hero fighting for the rights of the people, to his anti-aristocratic leanings, which were to sharpen within a few years to outspoken revolutionary sympathies. He completed the text in the first few months of his stay at Riga and started composing it before he left for Paris in 1839. There he finished the composition. But his hopes of having the work performed at the Paris Opéra proved in vain. *Rienzi* was first performed only in Dresden in 1842 and won him his first resounding success. Already on that occasion Wagner's proclivity for excessive length showed itself: the première started at six o'clock and lasted till after midnight. For a few performances the opera was given in two parts, entitled *Rienzi's Greatness* and *Rienzi's Fall*. However, as the public complained that they had to pay twice for what they could have heard at one sitting, the management decided to revert to playing the work as a single whole though with substantial cuts. In this form it remained for many years Wagner's most successful opera.

II

THE ROMANTIC OUTSIDER

1 Der fliegende Holländer

In the summer of 1839 Wagner, now 26 years of age, left Riga
for Paris. Hard-pressed by creditors, he secretly crossed the
Russian border and embarked in a small merchant vessel
bound for London. The impressions of this stormy voyage,
during which the ship was forced to shelter in a Norwegian
fiord, gave him the decisive impulse for *Der fliegende
Holländer (The Flying Dutchman)*. The idea of this subject
had already been in his mind for some time: he had come
across the story in Heine's *Salon*, published in 1834. There,
in the part entitled *From the Memoirs of Herr von Schnabelewopski*, Heine relates in detail the plot of a play he claims to
have seen in Amsterdam. (In fact, no such play has ever been
traced, which suggests that his version of the old legend was
Heine's own invention). In his *Autobiographical Sketch*,
Wagner gives full credit to Heine's share in his work:
"Particularly Heine's treatment of the redemption of that
Ahasuerus of the ocean, derived from a Dutch play of the
same title, provided me with everything for using this legend
as a subject for opera." (I, 17). He even adds that he discussed the project with the poet when visiting him in Paris.
(However, in his later full autobiography, *My Life*, he con-
siderably plays down his indebtedness to Heine).

Heine's account confirms beyond any doubt the decisive
part it played in the conception of the opera. The Dutch
captain of a ghostship that has roamed the seas from time

immemorial had once sworn by all the devils that he would sail around a promontory in a violent storm even if he were to sail until Judgment Day. The devil had taken him at his word, conceding that only the fidelity of a woman could redeem him. (Not believing in woman's fidelity, Heine adds cynically, the devil has allowed him to go ashore every seven years to take his chance—so far without luck). Once again seven years have passed, and the Dutchman goes ashore in Scotland where he makes friends with a Scots merchant and, on hearing of his beautiful daughter, offers him his treasures in return for her hand. At home, Katherina, the girl, contemplates a portrait of the Flying Dutchman, a family heirloom. When the captain enters, she is struck with the likeness. Concealing his true identity, he asks her to be his wife.

At this point Heine breaks off his account as his attention is diverted by a charming girl in the audience whom, on her overt invitation, he follows to a discreet rendez-vous. On his return to the theatre, he is just in time for the last scene, which shows the Dutchman's wife standing on a cliff wringing her hands, while her husband is seen on the deck of his ship. He is leaving her of his own free will as he has really fallen in love with her and does not wish her to share his fate. Whereupon she throws herself into the sea to prove that she is faithful unto death. The Flying Dutchman is redeemed and his ship disappears below the waves.

It is clear that Wagner has followed Heine's account closely. Originally he even intended to set the action in Scotland, but then, under the vivid impression of his short stay in a Norwegian fiord, he transferred the scene to Norway, turning the Scots merchant into a Norwegian captain, Daland. Moreover, he filled the gap Heine had whimsically left by introducing the figure of Erik, the girl's betrothed. This of course heightens the dramatic conflict and adds a new motive for the Dutchman's departure: it is by overhearing the pair and mistakenly suspecting the girl of infidelity that he now leaves her.

What attracted Wagner to this story was something deeper than his previous search for a suitable operatic subject. He

Der fliegende Holländer: production at the Lyceum Theatre, London, 1876, engraving by D. H. Friston.

saw in it a facet of a universal myth, comparing it to the travels of Odysseus and to the legend of the Wandering Jew with his longing for death and oblivion. No doubt he also felt it to be a poetic symbol of his own tempestuous life. "This (he writes in the *Communication to my Friends)* was the 'Flying Dutchman', who appeared to me repeatedly and with such irresistible fascination out of the morasses and billows of my life; it was the first folk-poem *(Volksgedicht)* which penetrated deep into my heart . . . From here begins my career as a *poet*, with which I abandoned that of a manufacturer of opera texts." (IV, 266). In a later passage he defines in greater detail the significance of this turning-point in his artistic development: "With *Rienzi* I merely intended to write an 'opera'; to this end, I looked for subjects and, only caring for 'opera', took them from ready-made literary works—a dramatic fairy-tale by Gozzi, a play by Shakespeare, finally a novel by Bulwer. In doing so, I did not advance formally beyond the skilful Lortzing, who also adapted ready-made plays for his opera texts. ★ . . . With *The Flying Dutchman,* I embarked on a new course by becoming myself the poet of a subject which existed only in the simple, raw outlines of a popular legend. From now on, I was with regard to all my dramatic works a *poet* in the first place, and became a musician once more only in the complete realisation of the poem." (IV, 316).

This self-interpretation throws a fascinating light on the way Wagner regarded both his own creative development and the interrelation between the poet and the musician in him. Looking back on *Der fliegende Holländer,* he is fully aware of its imperfections: "Much of it is still indecisive, the structure of the situations is still blurred, the poetic language and the verse still lack an individual stamp." (IV, 267).

No doubt *Der fliegende Holländer* is a transitional work. The juxtaposition of conventional opera, with its clearly defined arias, duets, and choruses, and a dramatic style foreshadowing the later works, is already apparent in the

---

★ Lortzing (1801–51), the composer of popular light operas, was in fact the first to write his own libretti, though without any ambition as a poet.

text. Long stretches of the dialogue are in traditional blank verse—a metre singularly unsuited to musical setting, which Wagner was still to employ in much of *Tannhäuser* and *Lohengrin*, and which, as he himself recognised later, was partly responsible for his slow, declamatory style. The musical numbers, on the other hand, are in shorter, rhymed verse, which naturally quickens the pulse of the music. For the first time, he also introduced his characteristic elemental cries—the "Hohoje! Hohoje" in the helmsman's song and the "Hui! Johohe" in Senta's ballad—which were to play such a significant part in the *Ring*. This unevenness of the language has its parallel in the delineation of the characters. Great care is lavished on the Dutchman and Senta, whose fateful involvement progresses with inevitable logic from their first encounter to the final catastrophe, whereas Daland and Erik are no more than stock-figures of conventional opera.

These two pairs move on altogether different planes: the Dutchman and Senta seem to live from the outset in a world of their own—foreshadowing the isolation of Tristan and Isolde in an alien world. It could be argued that the intervention of Erik and the misunderstanding to which it leads are not sufficient to motivate the Dutchman's departure. In fact there is no genuine dramatic conflict: Senta's resolve to sacrifice herself for the Dutchman is established from the very start, as expressed in her ballad, and the Dutchman never sees in her anything more than a means to his own salvation. Thus their union is from the outset indissolubly linked with the death-wish—another anticipation of *Tristan*. Before it finds expression in words, it is already established in the long silent look of recognition when they first set eyes on one another. Only once is Erik allowed to enter into the charmed circle in which Senta and the Dutchman move—it is, significantly, when he tells her of his dream which anticipates the whole drama about to unfold: the arrival of the Dutchman's ship, Senta's spontaneous surrender to the stranger, and even the ending: "And then—I saw you flee onto the sea!", whereupon Senta exclaims "in supreme ecstasy": "With him must I perish!"

Immediately after, the Dutchman enters . . .

In *Der fliegende Holländer*, Wagner established for the first time the dramatic structure he was to adhere to for the rest of his life—the condensation of the action in three acts—or, in his own words, "in three main situations of a drastic content." This structure is the basic form of all his mature works (with the single exception of *Das Rheingold*, which he conceived as a mere "Prelude" to the three *Ring* operas). Wagner did not achieve this form at a single stroke. To start with, he produced a draft for a one-act opera, to be given as a *lever de rideau* before a ballet. This he offered, with Meyerbeer acting as an intermediary, to the director of the Paris Opéra, Pillet, in the hope of gaining a foothold in that illustrious institute. Pillet agreed to accept his draft but added that he was obliged to commission some other composer to write the music. After lengthy negotiations, Wagner, as usual in dire financial straits, had to give in and sell his draft for the sum of 500 francs. (A French version, under the title *Le vaisseau fantôme*, was subsequently set to music by the choir master, Dietsch, and performed in 1842 with some success).

The 500 francs enabled Wagner to withdraw to the country and work out the full text himself, expanding it to three acts, to be performed without interruption. It is probably due to this genesis that it is the shortest of all his works (again, with the exception of *Das Rheingold*), keeping within the conventional limits of opera. He then composed the music within seven weeks, still in the vain hope of offering the work to the Paris Opéra. As it turned out it had its first performance only two years later in Dresden in 1843—with very moderate success.

Seen in the context of operatic history, *Der fliegende Holländer* looks both backwards and forwards. It still belongs to the tradition of romantic opera, with its interplay of the supernatural and human planes, its demonic hero, given to *Weltschmerz* and redeemed by a pure woman's love. It stands in a direct line with such operas as Weber's *Freischütz* and *Oberon*, Meyerbeer's *Robert le diable*, and Marschner's *Hans Heiling*. But it overshadows them all, not only by its sheer dramatic force and the genius of its music, but by the intense personal involvement of Wagner. The legendary figure of the Dutchman becomes his first symbolic self-portrait, he is flesh of his flesh, blood of his blood. He is—as Wagner felt himself to be—the typical romantic outsider, alienated from ordinary human society, trying in vain to lift the curse overhanging him through contact with another human being. It is Wagner's self-identification with his central character, more than anything else, which made him for the first time a poet, and which made *Der fliegende Holländer* the first truly Wagnerian opera in its complete fusion of drama and music. It is also the first of his works to centre on his dominant theme—*Erlösung* (the English "redemption" or "salvation", with their Christian connotations, are not really equivalent to the German term, which contains many more shades of meaning). From now on, this theme pervades nearly all his works, each time with different implications, from the romantic concept of redemption through a woman's self-sacrifice in *Der fliegende Holländer* and *Tannhäuser* to the wider significance it assumes in the *Ring*, in *Tristan*, and finally in *Parsifal*.

2 *Tannhäuser*

The two and a half years Wagner spent in Paris, with all their disappointments and frustrations, had one paradoxical result: they aroused in him a longing for Germany. "I experienced," he writes in retrospect, "a passionate, yearning patriotism of which I had previously no notion whatever." (XIII, 287). He emphasises that this newly awakened patriotism had no political implications. As there was little to attract him in contemporary Germany, his mind turned rather to the German past, above all to the Middle Ages. This was by no means an arbitrary personal choice: it coincided with the general trend of German thought, reflected in imaginative as well as historical writings and evoking the splendours of the past in contrast to the petty and oppressive conditions of the present. It was at this juncture that two books attracted Wagner's especial interest: the story of Tannhäuser, the medieval minstrel, and a history of the Hohenstaufen, the imperial dynasty at the height of the Middle Ages. These two books reflected the two directions in which Wagner was to move for some time—legend and history. For nearly a decade, these two aspects of the medieval world were in constant conflict in his mind, drawing him now towards the one, now towards the other.

At first history prevailed. Wagner's imagination was stirred by the figure of Frederick II, the most brilliant of the medieval emperors, known as "the wonder of the world", whose realm stretched from the Baltic to Sicily. In him Wagner saw "the supreme embodiment of the German ideal." However, he soon realised that this figure did not lend itself to operatic treatment. Instead his attention turned to the emperor's son Manfred, a somewhat weakish character, who ruled over only a small part of the empire, Apulia in southern Italy. Drawing partly on historical sources, partly on his own imagination, Wagner sketched out a drama in five acts under the title *Die Sarazenin* (*The Saracene Girl*). The action opens in Capua where Manfred holds his sumptuous court, surrounded by dancers and singers. He is challenged by a rebellious nobleman, Burello, who heads a hostile party disputing Manfred's authority. At this moment there appears a mysterious Saracene girl, Fatima, who has just arrived from her homeland, Palestine. Her inspired account of Manfred's father, the great Frederick, arouses Manfred from his indolence. Inspired by the girl, he makes his way to Luceria where he is enthusiastically acclaimed by the populace. Eventually he is crowned king in Naples. By this time he has fallen in love with Fatima: she, however, is pledged to marry a childhood friend, Nureddin, serving in Manfred's army. But Nureddin, incited by the conspirator, Burello, suspects the king of being his rival in love. As the procession leaves the cathedral, he tries to assassinate Manfred, but, held back by Fatima who cries out to the guards, he kills her instead. With her dying words she reveals to the king that she is his half-sister, a child of the emperor and a Saracene girl he had met in the Holy Land.

What attracted Wagner to this strange story was the clash between the German and the Mediterranean world, and the dominating figure of the great emperor whose spirit lived on in his daughter, the Saracene girl. However, he never worked out his draft fully. Most of the dialogue is still in sketchy prose, with some intermittent verse for arias and ensembles. Very soon *Die Sarazenin* was overshadowed by the other subject he had in mind—Tannhäuser. Wagner gives the reasons for this choice: "The former picture had been conjured up from outside; this figure sprang from my innermost being." (IV, 272). Evidently his heart was not in the subject, which might have thrown him back to grand opera in the style of *Rienzi*.

Even now the time for writing *Tannhäuser* had not yet come. Still in Paris, Wagner was approached by a resident German composer, Dessauer, requesting a libretto. In dire need of money for his return to Germany, Wagner agreed. Searching for a subject, he hit upon a tale by his favourite writer Hoffmann. Although it never got beyond a detailed prose sketch, *Die Bergwerke zu Falun (The Mines of Falun)* merits closer attention as it is much more in line with Wagner's development at this point than *Die Sarazenin*. Hoffmann's romantic story, set in the mining district of Falun in Sweden, tells of a young miner, Elis Fröhbaum, a former sailor who has been lured to the mines by a mysterious old man. One day, in the depth of the mountain, he comes face to face with the Mountain Queen. From that moment, he is torn between Ulla, a miner's daughter he hopes to marry, and the spell of the subterranean world. On the day of the wedding, he disappears into the mountain never to be seen again. Many years later his petrified body is found, and Ulla, now an old woman, recognises in him her lost bridegroom.

Wagner follows the story closely, dividing it into three acts. The only new character he introduces is a young sailor, Joens, who is also in love with Ulla. The first act opens on an assembly of the miners, presided over by Pehrsen, Ulla's father. Joens, who has just come home after a long absence at sea, extols the sailor's life. Presently Elis emerges from the pit and the two men greet one another as old shipmates. Somewhat distraught, Elis describes his encounter with a strange old man down the mine; at this Perhrsen relates the story of Old Torbern, a miner killed in a disaster a hundred years ago who is said to appear from time to time luring young miners on to rich veins. When Joens asks Pehrsen for his daughter's hand in marriage, Ulla consents half-heartedly, while Elis, secretly in love with her, rushes back to the mine heartbroken. The second act is set in the depth of the mountain. Elis, feeling betrayed, calls on Old Torbern to take him to the Mountain Queen he has once seen in a dream. The rock-wall opens and the Queen is revealed in all her glory. At this moment the voice of Ulla is heard from above, and shortly afterwards she appears followed by Joens and her father. Throwing herself into Elis's arms, she confesses her love for him, while Joens, who had been ignorant of her true feelings, generously surrenders her to his friend. In the last act, preparations for the wedding are in progress. On the morning of the wedding day Elis enters Ulla's room and tells her of a dream he has had of a precious stone hidden in the heart of the mountain: he is resolved to get it for her as a wedding gift. Ulla, fearing some misfortune, implores him not to go, but Elis tears himself away and disappears down the mine. The wedding guests arrive, there is singing and dancing, only the bridegroom is missing. Suddenly a dull crash is heard—the mine has collapsed. As miners try in vain to dig through the rubble, Ulla sinks "as if dead" to the ground. The mountain has taken Elis for ever.*

This story, with its blending of the human and the supernatural spheres, and its hero, another romantic outsider, torn between the two, obviously appealed to Wagner at this particular stage: it stands half-way between *Der fliegende Holländer* and *Tannhäuser* and might well have

* It is interesting to note that Hofmannsthal based his 5 act verse play *Das Bergwerk von Falun*, written in 1899, on Hoffman's tale, deepening its psychological and mystical implications.

served as a basis for another Wagner opera. However, it was designed for another composer and never went beyond the preliminary stage, since the draft was rejected by Pillet, the director of the Opéra, on the grounds that the décor of the second act would prove too cumbersome in view of the following ballet.

In April 1842, Wagner left Paris for Dresden. Passing through Thuringia, he caught sight of the Wartburg, its wooded hill. "The sight of the castle . . . affected me very deeply. I immediately identified a nearby hill-crest as Hörselberg and so constructed, travelling along in the valley, the setting for the third act of my *Tannhäuser.*" (XIV, 3).

However, the execution of this plan suffered a further delay. After his arrival in Dresden, Wagner was fully involved in the preparations for *Rienzi*, which had been accepted by the Court Opera. The conductor, Reissiger, himself a composer, begged Wagner to provide him with a suitable libretto. Anxious to humour him, Wagner promised to write one and bring a couple of pages to every piano rehearsal of *Rienzi*. He remembered the draft for *Die hohe Braut (The Noble Bride)* he had written six years before and sent to Scribe in Paris. Using this draft, he now expanded it into a full-scale libretto under the title *Die hohe Braut* or *Bianca und Guiseppe.*

The action is set in and around Nice in 1783, against the background of the French wars of revolution. The hero, Guiseppe, described as a huntsman, is in love with a nobleman's daughter, Bianca, who is betrothed against her will to an aristocrat, Count Rivoli. During a country dance, Guiseppe insists on dancing with the bride; at the Count's orders he is overwhelmed by soldiers but saved in the nick of time by Sormano, a noble brigand, who whisks him away to the mountains. Sormano (who has also been wronged by the Count) turns out to be the leader of a gang of rebels who are planning to attack the town with the help of the French. He persuades Guiseppe to join him, promising that Bianca will be his. But the assault fails, and both Guiseppe and Sormano are captured and imprisoned in a fortress under sentence of death. While the guards are drinking and singing outside the fortress, two friends enter disguised as hermits under the pretext of administering the last rites to the condemned. With their help the two prisoners don the hermits' garments and escape. In the fourth and final act, set in front of Nice cathedral, the wedding of Bianca and Count Rivoli is being celebrated. As the procession leaves the church Guiseppe stabs the Count, while the bride (who has taken poison) dies in his arms. At this moment the French burst through the gates of the city. Guiseppe, sword in hand, rushes off to fight them and is killed by the first shot.

This colourful plot Wagner furnished with all the paraphernalia of contemporary French and Italian opera, providing ample opportunities for musical devices, dances, soldiers' choruses, pilgrims' chants, drinking songs, battle music, and so on. Obviously this little work belonged, both in spirit and form, to a phase in his development which he had long left behind. That he was able and willing to complete it now only proves that he was prepared for anything that helped to further his own ends. As it turned out, Reissiger, who had commissioned it, never set it to music. Instead it was composed by one Johann Kittl, director of the Prague conservatoire, and performed in Prague in 1842 under the title *Die Franzosen vor Nizza (The French before Nice)*. A critic commented that the text confirmed Wagner's talent as a librettist, whereas his attempts at composition were merely an aberration.

Now at last Wagner was free to devote himself to *Tannhäuser*, which had ripened in his mind ever since his Paris days. He made the first draft in the summer of 1842 and completed the text by May 1843, when he was just thirty. The various sources he drew on have been studied exhaustively by critics and scholars. Wagner himself names four of them: first, a German *Volksbuch* of Tannhäuser, which he had come across in Paris—in fact, no such book has been traced; it is generally assumed that what Wagner was referring to was a collection of Thuringian legends by Ludwig Bechstein, published in 1835, containing not only the story of the 13th century minstrel but also that of *Sängerkrieg auf Wartburg (The Singers' Contest on the*

Wartburg). Secondly, there was a treatise by a Königsberg professor, Lucas, *Wartburgkrieg (The Wartburg Contest)*, published in 1838, which suggested that Tannhäuser was really a byname of another medieval poet, Heinrich von Ofterdingen, one of the competitors at the Wartburg song contest. Thirdly, there was a story by Tieck, *Der getreue Eckart und der Tannenhäuser (The faithful Eckart and Tannenhäuser)*, from his collection of fairy-tales, *Phantasus*; and fourthly, one of Hoffmann's tales from his *Serapions-brüder*, called *Der Kampf der Sänger (The Singers' Contest)*. To these may be added another potential source Wagner does not mention—Heine's poem *Der Tannhäuser*, first published in 1837 in his *Salon*—the same collection of writings from which he derived the idea of *Der fliegende Holländer*, and which no doubt was known to him. However, Heine's light-hearted treatment of the legend has little in common with Wagner's work.

Of these sources, it is worth looking more closely at Tieck's and Hoffmann's novellas, not only for their intrinsic interest but also because they had impressed themselves on Wagner since his early youth. Tieck's story is, like most of his writings, a rather confused amalgam of reality and dream, with a strong admixture of the pathological. In his version Tannenhäuser (he calls him by his original name) is a knight who one day disappears mysteriously from court. After many years his friend Friedrich sees him approaching in the garb of a pilgrim, his features strangely altered. At his request Tannenhäuser tells him his story: in despair over an unhappy love he had called upon the devil, who had shown him the way into the mountain known as the Venusberg. (According to legend, the pagan gods, with Venus at their head, had been banished there by the rise of Christianity, gathering round them their hellish hosts). Tannenhäuser goes on to describe in glowing colours the sensual delights of life in the mountain. One day, however, he was seized by a longing for "the old innocent earth". His wish was granted by God's mercy: he found himself back on earth and was now on the way to seek absolution from the Holy Father in Rome. Some months later, he returns, pale and barefoot, his pilgrim's garb in shreds: the Pope has not forgiven him and he is about to return to the Venusberg. Before disappearing for ever, he murders, in a fit of madness, his friend's wife, the very girl he had been in love with.

No doubt several ingredients of this story have contributed to Wagner's work: the vivid description of the Venusberg is clearly reflected in the music; the figure of Friedrich, Tannenhäuser's friend, foreshadows Wolfram, and even Friedrich's wife vaguely anticipates the figure of Elisabeth. However, there is no mention in Tieck's story of the singers' contest on the Wartburg.

This second strand of Wagner's opera is drawn from Hoffmann's tale *Der Kampf der Sänger*, which, in literary terms, is far superior to Tieck's. It depicts in vivid colours the 13th century court of the Landgrave of Thuringia who has gathered around him the most illustrious minstrels of his time to compete in song. Among them, Wolfframb von Eschinbach and Heinrich von Ofterdingen are the most outstanding. Both of them are in love with Countess Mathilde, a young widow at the court. Distressed by her coldness, Heinrich withdraws to neighbouring Eisenach, his hometown. One day, roaming through the woods, he meets a sinister stranger—evidently the devil—who advises him to take lessons from a famous magician and necromancer, Klingsohr, with whose help he will defeat all his rivals in song. After a long absence he returns to the court. At the singing contest he strikes up a song sounding "as though he was beating with powerful strokes on the dark gates of a strange, fateful realm and evoking mysteries of the unknown power dwelling there." He is crowned as victor by Mathilde, while Wolfframb, deeply disturbed by the song, warns Heinrich against the evil powers to which he has evidently succumbed. At the next contest all the singers, incensed by Heinrich's haughty bearing, turn against him, whereupon the Landgrave decrees that one of them, chosen by lot, shall challenge him in a public contest, and that Klingsohr (of whom he has been told by Heinrich) is to be the arbiter. The magician arrives, but the night before the contest he informs the Landgrave that a daughter has been born to the king of

Tannhäuser: miniature from the *Manessische Handschrift*, 13th century.

Hungary, called Elisabeth, who is destined to marry the Landgrave's son and will one day be canonised by the Pope on account of her piety. At that he departs, leaving the contest to take place without him. The lot of challenging Heinrich falls to Wolfframb. With his song in praise of pure love he wins the prize, loudly acclaimed by the people. Heinrich dissolves in a cloud of smoke, which suggest that one of Klingsohr's evil spirits had taken his place. The story ends happily with a letter Wolfframb receives from Heinrich, informing him that he has mended his ways and shaken off the evil spell.

It is easy to see that many aspects of this story are reflected in Wagner's opera: not only the colourful background of the Landgrave's court and the very names of the singers, but the contrast between Wolfframb's purity of heart and Heinrich's surrender to evil powers. The saintly Elisabeth, only incidentally mentioned by Hoffmann, becomes the Landgrave's niece and the object of both men's love. It may also be noted that several elements of Hoffmann's tale recur in *Die Meistersinger* (Hoffmann himself refers to the singers repeatedly as the "Meistersinger"): Heinrich von Ofterdingen, who with his daring song challenges the conventions of the contest, clearly foreshadows Walther von Stolzing; Mathilde, who crowns the winner and is the object of his love, seems like a first sketch of Eva; and lastly, it is the *Volk*, the people, who finally acclaim the winning song. It is also worth noting that Wagner may have encountered here for the first time the magician Klingsohr, who was to reappear many years later in his *Parsifal*.

These, then, are some of the sources which have contributed to *Tannhäuser*. In combining them in a unified action Wagner showed his supreme dramatic skill. His main achievement was of course to amalgamate the two separate legends of the Venusberg and the singers' contest by merging the figures of Tannhäuser and Heinrich von Ofterdingen (a trace of this can still be found in the Christian name of Heinrich which Wagner gave his hero). These two sources are still reflected in the double title of the opera: *Tannhäuser und der Sängerkrieg auf Wartburg (Tannhäuser and the Song*

Contest on the Wartburg). Originally, Wagner called the opera *Der Venusberg*. Only when he was warned by a friend that this name had given rise to ribald comments, especially on the part of medical students, did he change the title.

Wagner divides the action into three acts—the structure he had established in *Der fliegende Holländer*. Act I shows Tannhäuser in the Venusberg and his return to the world of men; Act II culminates in his clash with this world, represented by the Landgrave's court; in Act III we see him returning from Rome, his brief attempt to re-enter the Venusberg and his death. The whole drama turns on the duality of pagan sensuality and Christian purity. It is as though these opposites, separated in earlier works, now formed the basic conflict within a single drama, and indeed within the hero himself. Tannhäuser vacillates continually between the two extremes, embodied in Venus and Elisabeth. It was Wagner's supreme achievement to create the figure of Elisabeth as a counterpart to the pagan goddess. In the medieval poem it is Tannhäuser's invocation of Mary, the "pure virgin", which releases him from the snares of Venus. A trace of this can still be found in Tannhäuser's cry *Mein Heil liegt in Maria!* (My salvation lies in Mary!), at which the Venusberg vanishes at one stroke and he finds himself back on earth. By substituting Elisabeth for the Virgin, Wagner moves the action from the purely religious to the human plane. However, he still retains the wider implications of a struggle between Heaven and Hell. It is only by recognising that the Venusberg, in Christian eyes, was equated with Hell that the full significance of Tannhäuser's sin can be grasped. It is a sin for which there is no forgiveness, as is clearly stated in the words of the Pope:

> *Hast du so böse Lust geteilt,*
> *dich an der Hölle Glut entflammt,*
> *hast du im Venusberg geweilt:*
> *so bist nun ewig du verdammt!*

> (*If you have shared such evil lust,*
> *if Hell's fire has inflamed you,*

> *if you have dwelt in the Venusberg:*
> *you are damned for ever!)*

Tannhäuser's predicament can thus be compared to that of Faustus.

In his essay *Uber die Aufführung des 'Tannhäuser' (On the Staging of 'Tannhàuser')*, written in 1852, Wagner offers an illuminating interpretation of Tannhäuser's character. His most essential feature, he writes, is his wholehearted surrender to the situation he finds himself in and his abrupt change from one mood to another. "Tannhäuser is never and nowhere just 'a little' but everything fully and wholly." (V, 152). After surrendering wholeheartedly to the sensual charms of Venus, he is overwhelmed by nature in its pristine purity. When Wolfram utters the name of Elisabeth, it appears to him like "the shining star of a new life". Challenged by his rival singers, the representatives of social convention, he responds with his outrageous song in praise of sensual love. With deep contrition he sets out for Rome, returning in utter despair when forgiveness is denied him. In short, one may add, Tannhäuser's nature is that of the romantic artist, forever vacillating between extremes of emotion. No doubt he, like the Flying Dutchman before him, bears traits of Wagner himself. He, too, is a romantic outsider, an outcast from human society, marked by a curse. But while in *Der fliegende Holländer* the cause of this curse—the invocation of the Devil—is never mentioned but taken for granted as a familiar part of the legend, we see it here visibly enacted in Tannhäuser's association with Venus. And as with the Dutchman, there is one redeeming feature pervading his whole being—his longing for salvation. Amidst the delights granted him by the goddess, Tannhäuser yearns for suffering:

> *Nicht Lust allein liegt mir am Herzen;*
> *aus Freuden sehn' ich mich nach Schmerzen.*

> (*I care not for lust alone,*
> *in my joy I yearn for pain*)

Tannhäuser: the first production, Dresden, 1845, drawing by T. Tischbein.

It is this yearning which drives him back to the human world and to Elisabeth. "This deep human longing," Wagner writes, "was for the woman who suffers with him, whereas Venus only enjoyed herself with him." (V, 154). But this longing is really, deep down, a death-wish. As Tannhäuser expresses it in his entreaty to Venus to let him go:

> O Göttin, woll' es fassen,
> mich drängt es hin zum Tod.

> (Oh goddess, understand,
> it drives me on to death)

With this longing for death as the only way of deliverance (Erlösung) from unforgivable sin, Tannhäuser is related not only to the Flying Dutchman but also to Tristan and, ultimately, to Amfortas.

The other characters, unlike those in Der fliegende Holländer (with the exception, of course, of Senta), are by no means operatic stereotypes. Each is fully individualised, and each is involved in the drama of the protagonist. Wolfram, his friend, is the obvious foil to Tannhäuser; manly, upright, noble-hearted. Their contrast is most clearly reflected in their respective songs in praise of love: while Wolfram glorifies spiritual love, likening it to a distant star in heaven, Tannhäuser extols fleshly lust, as Venus has taught him. There are subtle hints that Wolfram, too, is in love with Elisabeth, but from the beginning resigns this love out of friendship for Tannhäuser. For stronger than anything separating the two men is Wolfram's unfaltering loyalty. It is he who, by reminding Tannhäuser of Elisabeth, brings him back to the court; it is he who, in the third act, anxiously waits for his return from Rome and, when Tannhäuser is resolved to re-enter the Venusberg, holds him back. Once more it is by pronouncing the name of Elisabeth that he finally saves his friend.

As for Elisabeth, it would be wrong to regard her as no more than a personification of saintliness. She, too, undergoes development in the course of the drama. In her great scene with Tannhäuser, she admits that his song has aroused in her "a strange new life":

> *Gefühle, die ich nie empfunden!*
> . *Verlangen, das ich nie gekannt!*

> (*Emotions I have never felt!*
> *Longings I have never known!*)

Only when he reveals that he has been in the Venusberg does she feel he has struck her "a deadly blow". Yet she shields him with her body from the outraged knights, imploring them to let him seek salvation through atonement. From that moment she renounces earthly love and becomes a mere intermediary, prepared to give her life for his salvation. This new role is movingly expressed in her prayer to the Virgin in which she abjures all "sinful desire" and asks forgiveness for *his* guilt. In the end it is through her vicarious death that Tannhäuser is saved, symbolised by the staff putting forth green shoots. The role of Elisabeth is thus similar to Senta's: like the Flying Dutchman, Tannhäuser is redeemed through a woman's self-sacrifice. It is significant that he attains his salvation not through the Church (represented by the Pope) but through the compassion of another human being.

In terms of structure and language *Tannhäuser* marks a great advance on *Der fliegende Holländer*. Though there are still well-defined ensembles and arias, they are far better integrated into the dramatic action. Moreover, most of the songs are dramatically justified as parts of the singing contest. The dialogue, too, though still largely in blank verse, is terser and more swift moving.

Tannhäuser is Wagner's first consciously German opera. Significantly, it was first conceived in Paris, growing out of his intense longing for Germany. This origin can still be felt in the evocation of the Thuringian landscape, the pure simplicity of the shepherd's song, in striking contrast to the hot-house atmosphere of the Venusberg. It is perhaps no mere coincidence that it was just the Venusberg scene which Wagner expanded in the Paris version of 1861.

The score of *Tannhäuser* was completed in April 1845. Exhausted by the strain of this work as well as by his activities as Royal Kapellmeister at the Dresden opera, Wagner spent the summer at the Bohemian spa of Marienbad. As it turned out, this Marienbad summer proved one of the most fruitful periods of his life. Stimulated no doubt by his preoccupation with the figure of Wolfram von Eschenbach, he immersed himself in the epic *Parzival* and began "to converse with Parzival and Titurel in that strange and yet so intensely homely poem." (XIV, 115). The time for this subject was still far off, but the occupation with the Grail myth led him to the related legend of Lohengrin, which affected him with "an alarmingly growing excitement". For the moment, he resisted the temptation to become involved in this subject, fearing that its tragic implications might affect his health. Instead he conceived the plan for a "light"comic opera which would be related to *Tannhäuser* as the satyr play was to Greek tragedy. No doubt the potentially humorous aspects of a song contest impressed themselves on his mind. In short, he conceived the plan of *Die Meistersinger*. Within a few days he produced a prose draft containing the plot of the opera in every detail but for the names of the characters, with the exception of Hans Sachs, David and Magdalene. At the end of this draft, he wrote the two verses which, slightly altered, were to conclude *Die Meistersinger*:

> *Zerging' das heilige römische Reich in Dunst,*
> *Uns bliebe doch die heilige deutsche Kunst.*

> (*Though the Holy Roman Empire dissolve in mist,*
> *There still remains for us holy German art.*)

However, he realised that the time for this work had not yet come. As he put it in retrospect: the kind of humour with which he approached the subject was merely "irony". It was not yet the warm, all-embracing humour, rooted "in life itself", which only ripeness can bring. Another sixteen years were to pass before Wagner reached that stage. In short, during that summer of 1845 the seeds were sown for all his future works with the exception of *Tristan* and the *Ring*.

3 *Lohengrin*

In the event, it was *Lohengrin* which attracted Wagner with irresistible force. Wagner first encountered the legend in Paris, in the same volume that contained the story of the Wartburg singing contest. Another influence was Wolfram von Eschenbach's epic *Parzival,* which ends with the story of Parzival's son Loherangrin. The decisive impulse, however, came from the 13th century anonymous epic on that subject. Only when Wagner came to know the legend in this form, as a "genuine folk poem", did *Lohengrin* take shape in his mind.

No other work (with the exception of the *Ring*) received from Wagner such extensive comment as this, with regard to its intrinsic meaning as well as to its autobiographical significance. He saw his *Lohengrin* in close connection with its predecessor: in *Tannhäuser,* he writes in *A Communication,* he had longed to extricate himself from a frivolous sensuality—"the only expression of sensuality the present age knows"—towards "the pure, the chaste, the virginal". Now that he had attained this height, he felt himself to be alone, "outside the modern world". (IV, 294). But from this lonely height, he was longing for "the woman" as the ultimate fulfilment. It was the same longing that had impelled the Flying Dutchman and driven Tannhäuser from the depth of the Venusberg in search of purity, embodied in Elisabeth.

This line of thought is not only characteristic of Wagner's propensity to self-interpretation and self-dramatisation, it also reflects current ideas of the period—the antithesis of sensual and spiritual love and the idealisation of woman. Above all, it bears out the intensity of Wagner's personal involvement in this as in all his mature works. Like the Flying Dutchman and Tannhäuser, Lohengrin is an embodiment of the romantic outsider, in other words, of the artist who feels himself to be aloof from the ordinary world of men. What separates him from this world is not, as with the Dutchman and Tannhäuser, a curse, but on the contrary his elevated status as a member of the community of the Grail.

So, instead of seeking salvation through the self-sacrificing love of a woman, he descends from his elevated position to answer a woman's cry for help. Nevertheless, his demand for unquestioning surrender is no less exacting. In spite of these reversed roles, the basic conflict between the outsider and human society remains the same. Baseness and envy instil their poison into the heart of the loving woman; doubt in his mission extracts from him the revelation of his divine origin and forces him to return to his seclusion.

One can see to what extent Wagner conceived the Lohengrin legend in his own image. He was not concerned with its original Christian connotations: the holy Grail, which stands at the centre of *Parsifal*, plays merely an ephemeral role. He sees the story rather as part of a timeless myth which appears in many variations throughout the ages. Just as he compared the Flying Dutchman to Odysseus, so he now finds a Greek equivalent to the Lohengrin legend in the myth of Zeus and Semele: the god approaches Semele in human guise; filled with suspicion, she begs him to appear in his true shape, and Zeus is forced to fulfil her wish although he knows the sight must destroy her. "He carries out his own death sentence," Wagner concludes, "when the brilliance of his divine appearance destroys the beloved." (IV, 290).

In keeping with the medieval epic, Wagner sets the scene in Brabant in the first half of the 10th century at the time of the Saxon king known as Henry the Fowler. Thus he boldly combines myth and history, very much as he does in *Tannhäuser*. But while in the latter the two spheres— Venusberg and the Landgrave's court—are separated, they merge in *Lohengrin*. The historical background is clearly defined: a Hungarian invasion threatens from the East and the German king has come to Brabant to summon the nobles in defence of the country. Thus on one hand, we have a historical grand opera, with its traditional devices of festive processions, trumpet calls, rousing ensembles; on the other, the myth of the Grail-knight with his fairy-tale swan and all its attendant miracles.

Wagner's main achievement in transforming the original epic into drama is the introduction of Ortrud as the motive force of the whole action. It is she who incites her husband Telramund to charge Elsa with the murder of her brother; it is she who instils doubt in Elsa's heart, thus leading her to the fatal question; and it is she, as she finally reveals, who has turned the brother into a swan. (Admittedly this invisible transformation of Gottfried and his re-appearance at the end, only rarely understood by the audience, constitute one of the weaker links in the plot.) By making Ortrud the chief agent, Wagner has diminished the role of Telramund, who becomes little more than a tool in his wife's hand. Their relationship recalls, in some respects, that of Macbeth and Lady Macbeth. On the other hand, Wagner has added a new dimension to the drama by making Ortrud a worshipper of the old Teutonic gods. Thus her hatred of Lohengrin, and her use of Elsa to frustrate his mission, assume the wider aspects of a struggle between paganism and Christianity. Moreover the Teutonic gods are here conceived as evil powers—very unlike the role they play in the *Ring*. This is strikingly expressed in Ortrud's invocation of the gods to assist her in her treacherous schemes:

> *Wodan! Dich Starken rufe ich!*
> *Freia! Erhab'ne, höre mich!*
> *Segnet mir Trug und Heuchelei!*
> *dass glücklich meine Rache sei!*

> (I call thee, strong Wodan!
> Hear me, high Freia!
> Bless my deceit and falsehood
> that my revenge may succeed!)

Ortrud is contrasted to Elsa as night is to day. The scene between the two—the pivotal scene of the whole drama—has a Shakespearean touch in its visual manifestation: at first, Ortrud below in the dark—Elsa, all in white, on the balcony; then, when Elsa has led her up, the two women on an equal level, with Ortrud gradually gaining the upper hand.

Elsa is obviously a direct successor to Senta and Elisabeth—the embodiment of purity and total devotion to the man she loves. Her vision of the knight who will come to save her has its parallel in Senta's ballad, and her ecstatic recognition when she first sets eyes on Lohengrin equals the first wordless encounter between Senta and the Dutchman. Her gradually deepening doubt, after Ortrud has roused her suspicion, is revealed by degrees—a masterstroke of psychological insight. At the end of Act II, her love still overrules all possible doubt:

> Hoch über alles Zweifels Macht
> . . . soll meine Liebe stehn!

> (High above all power of doubt
> . . . shall stand my love!)

Then, in the crucial scene in the bridal chamber, her urge to ask the fatal question increases step by step: at first she begs Lohengrin to impart to her his secret only out of fear that some danger may threaten him which she wants to share. When Lohengrin tells her in good faith that her love must compensate him for the splendours he has left behind, she cries out in dread that one day he may long to go back. Finally, imagining she can see the swan coming to take him away, she formulates the forbidden question—"and though it cost my life!" The tragedy is that all along her urge to know his name and origin springs from the intensity of her love.

The tragedy is Elsa's rather than Lohengrin's. To all appearance, the Grail-knight is a static figure, "the knight in shining armour", as Elsa sees him (in lichter Waffen Scheine)—a phantasm of the romantic imagination rather than a person of flesh and blood. A certain coldness attaches to him throughout. Both on his arrival and departure, his prime concern is for the swan who has brought him rather than for the woman he has come to protect and eventually to marry. Only in the second act, in the long dialogue in the bridal chamber, does he open his heart and reveal some human feeling, declaring that, though he had never seen Elsa, love guided him to her:

> Die nie sich sah'n, wir hatten uns geahnt:
> war ich zu deinem Streiter auserlesen,
> hat Liebe mir den Weg zu dir gebahnt.

(We who have never met, were aware of one another:
Though I was chosen to be your champion,
love guided me to you)

Again, in the third act, after he has revealed his name before the whole assembly, he turns to Elsa "with the most painful emotion":

O Elsa! Was hast du mir angetan?
Als meine Augen dich zuerst ersahn,
zu dir fühlt' ich in Liebe mich entbrannt,
und schnell hatt' ich ein neues Glück erkannt . . .

(Oh Elsa! What have you done to me?
When first I set eyes on you
I felt inflamed with love for you
and quickly recognised a new happiness . . .) *

There is one final gesture which shows Lohengrin's human concern: when he has addressed the swan for the last time, he turns to Elsa, handing her his horn, sword, and ring to give to her young brother. One can't help feeling that in this bequest there is a faint suggestion of a child that was never to be:

Doch bei dem Ringe soll er mein gedenken,
der einstens dich aus Schmach und Not befreit!

(. . . But by the ring he shall remember me
Who once saved you from shame and from distress!)

---

* In the original version of this passage, Wagner went even further: Lohengrin continues:

Nun muss ich ewig Reu' und Busse tragen,
weil ich von Gott zu dir mich hingesehnt,
denn ach, der Sünde muss ich mich verklagen,
dass Weiberlieb' ich göttlich rein gewähnt!   (XII, 357)

(Now I must bear for ever penance and remorse
because my longing turned from God to you,
for, alas! I must charge myself with the sin
of having thought woman's love divinely pure!)

No doubt, Wagner felt that this would introduce a new idea which might impair the flawless image of the knight.

Lohengrin: departure of the swan knight, engraving after
Wilhelm Kaulbach, 1866.

Evidently Wagner himself felt that the coldness which attaches to his hero, above all, his seemingly heartless departure at the end, might forfeit the sympathy of the audience. Perturbed by the criticism of some friends who found Elsa's punishment too harsh, he seriously considered giving the story a different ending: Elsa might leave together with Lohengrin "for some kind of atonement which would remove her, too, from the world." (XIV, 147). He even drafted a solution according to which Lohengrin would resign his superior status in order to stay with Elsa. Soon, however, he realised that the original tragic ending was the only one possible.

The text of *Lohengrin* represents a further step in the direction of music drama. Despite the numerous choral ensembles, required by the action, musical numbers and dramatic dialogue are almost fully integrated.* The language is more differentiated, and, for long stretches, Wagner employs short rhymed verse instead of his former iambic pentameters, which has the effect of quickening the pace. The three-act structure shows for the first time a pattern that was to recur in *Tristan* as well as in *Die Meistersinger*: day-night-day. In short, *Lohengrin*, which concludes the first part of Wagner's creative life, is both the culmination of romantic opera in the traditional sense and the opening of the way which was to lead him to new, as yet only dimly perceived forms.

Wagner wrote the text of *Lohengrin* in the autumn of 1845, immediately after the first Dresden performance of *Tannhäuser*, and spent the next two years composing the music. He completed the score in March 1848; a few weeks before, revolution had broken out in Paris, spreading rapidly to Germany and Austria.

---

* When Wagner read the completed text to a small circle of friends, Schumann, who was among the audience, objected that it didn't offer any opportunities for musical numbers. "For fun", Wagner writes, "I read him some bits of my poem in the form of arias and cavatinas, whereupon he smilingly declared himself satisfied." (XIV, 147)

III

FROM HISTORY TO MYTH

1848, the year of European revolution, was also a crucial year in Wagner's intellectual and artistic development. The two are closely related. Wagner's active participation in the uprising, which subsequently forced him into exile, was inspired largely by his revolutionary ideas on the function of the theatre in modern society and his acute sense of alienation from the contemporary world of opera—in short, it had predominantly artistic and personal origins. The connection between social and artistic revolution is the theme running through the large body of theoretical writings of the next few years. In *A Communication to my Friends* Wagner sums it up in the following words: "Reflecting on the possibility of a fundamental change in our theatrical conditions, I was driven quite automatically to a full realisation of the worthlessness of the political and social conditions . . . This realisation was decisive for the whole development of my further life." (IV, 308).

The various dramatic projects Wagner conceived in that crucial year are linked in one way or another with current revolutionary ideas. They centred on two apparently unconnected subjects, one historical, the other mythological: Frederick Barbarossa and—Siegfried. Wagner was fully aware of the significance of these alternatives: "Once more, and for the last time, I was faced with myth and history, and this time I was even urged to decide whether I should write a musical drama or a spoken play."(IV, 311). He goes on to reflect that both projects had actually sprung from the same source—his search for "the true man", that is, "youthfully beautiful man in the exuberant freshness of his strength." (IV, 311–312). He saw this idea embodied both in the mythical figure of Siegfried and in the Holy Roman Emperor Frederick I, known as Barbarossa. Though the two plans went side by side, he first turned to the historical theme of Frederick, which seemed to him more closely related to the actual aspirations of the revolution*

Although these aspirations ranged over a wide spectrum from democratic liberalism to communism, they also included a strong monarchic trend, culminating in the idea of a *Volkskaiser*, a popular emperor.** This idea was romantically linked in the popular mind with the 12th century Hohenstaufen Emperor, who, according to legend, sat sleeping within a mountain, only to wake when the *Volk* should be in need of him. It was under the influence of these ideas that Wagner turned to the Emperor who had died on his way to the Holy Land after a life-long struggle against the power of the Church.

Friedrich Rotbart, of which only a prose draft survives, is in fact one of the few works Wagner conceived from the outset as a spoken play. Turning it into an opera would have thrown him back, he felt, to the period of *Rienzi*, which he had left behind for good. The play revolves round the struggle between the two warring factions, the Ghibellines and the Guelfs, headed respectively by the Emperor Frederick I and the Duke of Saxony, Henry the Lion. Written "in popular rhymed verse in the style of our Middle High German epic poets", it was to be in five acts: Act I—Diet of the Roncalian Fields, assertion of supreme imperial power; Act II—Siege and capture of Milan; Act III—Defection of Henry the Lion and Frederick's defeat at Lignano; Act IV—Diet of Augsburg, humiliation and banishment of Henry; Act

---

* In fact, he had conceived this plan as early as 1846, during his work on *Lohengrin*.

** The relationship between republicanism and monarchy is the subject of one of Wagner's political essays, published in June, 1848, *Wie verhalten sich republikanische Bestrebungen dem Königtum gegenüber? (How do republican aspirations stand in relation to monarchy?)*

V—Court festivities at Mainz, peace with the Lombards, reconciliation with the Pope, news of the fall of Jerusalem, and departure for the Holy Land. Of these five acts, only Acts I and II are sketched in some detail, without offering any clues as to the dramatic content beyond some speeches of the Emperor on the struggle between temporal and spiritual power. However, Wagner soon realised that the vast subject far exceeded the limits of a play. Or, as he explained: man, in his historical context, was determined by social and political circumstances instead of determining them. Pursuing this line of thought, he once more turned to myth, where man is "free creator of circumstances". These reflections on the interrelation of history and myth gave rise to an extensive treatise, which not only illuminates the ideas underlying the abandoned play but is a landmark on Wagner's road to myth.

Die Wibelungen, subtitled *World History out of Saga,* is a curious conglomeration of historical and mythological ideas, partly derived from current romantic conceptions, partly from Wagner's own speculations. Two lines of thought intermingle: firstly, the idea of imperial power, which has its origin in the *Urkönigtum,* the ancient kingship of prehistoric Germanic tribes, and achieved its supreme realisation in the Frankish dynasty known under the name of Ghibellines or Wibelingen (Wagner has a facile etymological explanation for the merging of the two names and his own *Wibelungen);* secondly, the saga of the Nibelungen, centring on the heroic figure of Siegfried and his fight for the *Hort,* the hoard which is the symbol of unlimited worldly power. Since one of the Frankish dynasties, residing on the Lower Rhine, bore the legendary name of Nibelungen, there is a mythical identity between them and the Nibelungen of the saga—in other words, the aspirations of the Frankish kings to imperial power has its mythical parallel in the struggle for the hoard. The first historical figure to claim world power was Charlemagne; after him, "he who won the imperial crown deemed himself to be the true owner of the hoard." (II, 142).

The last great dynasty to aspire to this power were the Hohenstaufen, with Frederick Barbarossa as their first towering figure. Wagner describes in greater detail Barbarossa's struggle against the Pope and the opposing faction of the Guelfs, and his setting out for the Third Crusade on which he died. He even manages to bring in the legend of the Holy Grail, "the ideal representative and successor to the Nibelungen hoard". Striving for the Grail now takes the place of the struggle for the hoard, which gradually degenerates to "real property" in the modern world. Following this line of thought, Wagner arrives at a condemnation of hereditary wealth and the inequality of contemporary society. But "the poor people" go on believing in the existence of the hoard, which has returned inside a mountain "like that from which Siegfried once won it from the Nibelungen". The great Emperor had taken it there to preserve it for better times. "There he sits now, old Barbarossa Frederick; around him the treasures of the Nibelungen, at his side the sharp sword which once struck down the grim dragon." (II, 155). This identification of Frederick with Siegfried culminates in the revolutionary challenge which concludes the essay: "When will you return, Frederick, you glorious Siegfried! and strike the evil, gnawing dragon of humanity?" (XII, 229). This strange and somewhat confused treatise is interesting for two reasons: it is Wagner's last theoretical attempt at merging history and myth (as he had done in *Tannhäuser* and *Lohengrin*), and it contains his first extensive reference to the Nibelungen Saga. It was followed almost immediately by another prose piece entitled *Der Nibelungen-Mythus (The Nibelung Myth)*—no less than the first comprehensive draft of his tetralogy. In this draft, he severs all links with history and penetrates to pure myth: Barbarossa has finally yielded to Siegfried. For it is Siegfried, the mythical embodiment of "true man", who stands at the centre of the saga and attracts Wagner's attention in the first place. Although he continued the whole action of his later tetralogy, he first considered only its tragic conclusion as a subject for a music drama. Immediately following his draft of *Der Nibelungen-Mythus* he wrote the text for a "Grand Heroic Opera in 3 Acts" *Siegfrieds Tod (Siegfried's Death)* covering roughly the action of *Götterdämmerung*. However, it took another three years before he returned to the subject, extending it backwards by adding *Der junge Siegfried (Young Siegfried)* and a further year before he completed all four dramas. This whole creative process will be traced in detail when the genesis of the *Ring* is considered.

Immediately after completing *Siegfrieds Tod* Wagner embarked on a very different subject—Jesus of Nazareth. In his *Communication to my Friends,* he gives an account of the mental state he found himself in at the time, which drew him to the figure of Christ. His revulsion at the state of public affairs had driven him more and more into isolation; the first performance of *Lohengrin,* planned by the Dresden Opera for the autumn of 1848, had been cancelled on the grounds of his public revolutionary activities. "This sad, lonely position as an artist . . . I could only overcome by satisfying my restless urge for new projects. I felt impelled to write something that would convey this painful awareness in a manner intelligible to present day life." (IV, 331). Thus his preoccupation with the story of Christ grew out of a deep personal involvement. He identified Christ's rejection of the corrupt Roman world with his own rebellion against contemporary society. In short, he used the story of the human Jesus—as opposed to the divine—as a medium for his own feelings of isolation and revolt.

Of all these thoughts, little can actually be traced in the extensive prose scenario Wagner wrote for his projected drama *Jesus von Nazareth*; in fact, this scenario keeps close to the Scriptures, dividing the action into five acts. Here is a brief synopsis of his plan: Act I: Tiberias in Galilee. The house of the tax collector Levi. Judas Iscariot and Barabbas in conversation. Barabbas intends to lead a revolt against the Romans; Judas tells him of Jesus, hoping he will be elected king of the Jews. Jesus arrives, followed by a crowd, and restores Levi's daughter to life. Mary Magdalene is brought in to be stoned as an adulteress. Jesus saves her and preaches his gospel of love.

Act II: At the Lake of Gennesaret; Jesus, his mother Mary and Mary Magdalene. Jesus speaks of his youth, his baptism, the temptation in the wilderness. To escape from the crowd, who want to make him king, he boards a ship and speaks to them.

Act III: Scene i: The Council House. Pilate and Caiaphas. The rebellion led by Barabbas has been crushed, and Barabbas has been sentenced to death. Caiaphas warns of fresh upheavals in Galilee, led by Jesus. A Pharisee suggests that they win over Judas.

Scene ii: Square in front of the Temple. Jesus' entry on a mule, acclaimed by the crowd. He drives the money changers from the Temple. The Pharisees rouse the crowd against him. One of them wins over Judas, overheard by Mary Magdalene.

Act IV: Scene i: The Last Supper. Mary Magdalene anoints Jesus, who prepares the disciples for his death.

Scene ii: The Garden of Gethsemane. The disciples fall asleep; Jesus alone. The soldiers arrive, led by Judas, and take Jesus away, while the disciples flee in all directions.

Act V: Square before Pilate's Palace. Roman soldiers lying around a fire. Peter's betrayal. Jesus is brought out of the Palace, interrogated by Pilate. After being mocked by the soldiers, he is led away to be crucified. The sky darkens, earthquake. John and the two Marys return and tell of his death. Finally, Peter announces to the crowd the fulfilment of Jesus' message. All gather around him, asking to be baptised. End.

This in brief outline is Wagner's plan, filled in with a wealth of detail. The few indications of dialogue are partly derived from the Gospels, partly his own invention. The most noteworthy addition is the major role allotted to Barabbas as the leader of an abortive revolt against the Romans, which gives greater significance to the crowd clamouring for his release. More illuminating than this scenario is an extensive commentary Wagner has added to it. This commentary, though frequently referring to passages from the Gospels, is only loosely linked to the subject. Instead it contains his own reflections on various topics, centring around two antithetical key-words—Law and Love. Love is the Law of Life for all creation. But man has created Law to limit Love, in order to protect the three mainstays of society, power, property, and marriage. In doing so he has sinned against the primary law of his own free life. By protecting property he has established the inequality of society; by protecting marriage he has constrained the very essence of love. Free love can realise itself only outside the law, that is, against the law. "But Love is mightier than the Law, it is the primary law *(das Urgesetz)* of life". (XI, 306). This, reduced to its essence, is the gist of Wagner's argument.* Although he links his ideas again and again with specific sayings of Christ, they encompass a much wider range, pointing to some of the basic concepts underlying the *Ring*. (It must be borne in mind that his key-word, *Liebe*, denotes every shade of meaning from sexual passion to charity in the Christian sense.) The antithesis of Law and Love constitutes, as we shall see, the central conflict of the whole tetralogy.

Seen in this light, the two dramatic projects Wagner conceived side by side, *Jesus von Nazareth* and *Siegfried*, are not as incompatible as they seem at first sight. Both were destined, as Wagner expressly states, for "the ideal stage of the future". But while the Jesus drama was soon abandoned, *Siegfried* went on germinating, until it found full realisation in *Der Ring des Nibelungen*. Yet his passing pre-occupation with the figure of Christ and the world of the Gospels finally bore fruit in *Parsifal*. The description of Mary Magdalene anointing Jesus clearly prefigures Kundry and Parsifal.

Jesus von Nazareth, on which Wagner worked at the beginning of 1849, was in his own words, "his last artistic occupation" in Germany. For the next few months he lived in a state of restless expectation. In May the revolution broke out in Dresden. Wagner's involvement in the uprising, his escape after it was crushed by Prussian troops, and his headlong flight to Switzerland are well-known facts of his biography. Overnight he found himself in exile, which was to last for fifteen years.

---

* The influence on Wagner's thought of the philosopher Ludwig Feuerbach and the Russian anarchist Bakunin, his close associate during those Dresden days, has been acknowledged by Wagner himself.

During these fateful weeks he pondered on new dramatic projects. On the eve of the Dresden uprising, walking between the barricades, he worked out in his mind "the material for a drama *Achilleus,* which had occupied me for some time." (XIV, 240). Very little survives of this plan, but the very fact that Wagner considered it is significant in many respects. From his early youth he had been deeply interested in Greek antiquity. This interest was revived by a production of Gluck's *Iphigenia in Aulis* in 1846, for which he revised both the text and the music, bringing them closer to Euripides' play. Soon after, while working on *Lohengrin,* he immersed himself in Greek drama, above all in Aeschylus' *Oresteia.* "Nothing was like the sublime emotion (he writes in *My Life*) which the *Agamemnon* aroused in me: until the end of the *Eumenides* I remained in a state of rapture from which I have never really quite become reconciled to modern literature. My ideas about the meaning of drama, and particularly of the theatre, were formed decisively by these impressions." (XIV, 169). This is amply borne out by the dominant role Wagner assigns to the drama and theatre of ancient Greece in his theoretical writings. Moreover, his admiration for Aeschylus' trilogy was an important element in his conception of a tetralogy on the Nibelung myth.

His attraction to the figure of Achilles had its special reasons. Wagner saw in him no doubt the Greek counterpart to Siegfried, the supreme hero, half human, half of divine descent. The few surviving notes to this dramatic project emphasise this aspect: "Achilles rejects the immortality his mother Thetis offers him . . . His mother recognises that Achilles is greater than the elements (the gods)." And: "Man is the perfection of God. The eternal Gods are the elements that engender Man. Thus creation finds its completion in Man. Achilles is superior to and more complete than the elemental Thetis." (XII, 283).

These reflections show the distinct influence of Feuerbach's anthropocentric philosophy, which conceives Man as the summit and purpose of creation: *homo homini deus.* They point to the common ground of three such diverse subjects as Siegfried, Jesus, and Achilles: all three figures are embodiments of "God turned Man", or heroes in the supreme sense as Wagner conceived it.

The plan for an Achilles drama was soon dropped. But as late as 1865 Wagner still mentions it in a letter to King Ludwig. Of the three spheres he approached almost simultaneously—the Germanic, the Biblical, and the Greek —he reverted finally to the Germanic. But it was not yet the Nibelung myth. Instead he turned to another Nordic saga, *Wieland der Schmied (Wieland the Smith)*. As always, the choice of subject sprang from a deep personal involvement: the story of the mythical smith who, held in bondage by a cruel king, forges himself wings to regain his freedom, seemed to Wagner a symbol of his own predicament. Of all the projects of that period, this one came closest to completion. During the first few months of his exile in Zürich, he worked out a detailed prose draft complete with dialogue. As the plan of a Wieland opera competed for quite some time with the Nibelungen, it is well worth looking at more closely.

The scene is set in Norway, in the land of the Vikings. Wieland is sitting at his forge on the sea shore, a free man, fashioning jewellery for himself and his two brothers. Suddenly he sees three swans flying out to sea, one of which seems injured. As it drops into the sea, Wieland swims out and brings it ashore. He carefully detaches the wings and finds a beautiful maiden—Schwanhilde. She tells him of her descent from the Lichtalben, the gods of the upper air, and how she has been wounded in her fight against King Neiding. Wieland falls in love with her and promises to cure her; in return, Schwanhilde gives him a ring which has the power to arouse love and bring victory to its owner. Wieland accepts the ring, but, protesting that he does not need it, hangs it up at his door. Then he leads her into his house and goes to tell his brothers what has happened. Unseen by him, a ship has arrived carrying King Neiding's daughter Bathilde, who has followed Schwanhilde, intent on gaining her magic ring. Seeing the ring at the door, she takes it. A second ship brings Gram, the king's marshal, sent to seize Wieland and take him back to the court. While some of the men go in search of the smith, others set his house on fire. Wieland is brought back in chains and, seeing his house in flames, calls in vain for Schwanhilde. With the help of his brothers, he drives Gram's men back to the ship. They sail away while Wieland stays behind in despair. Then he sets out to avenge the death of Schwanhilde.

Act II is set at King Neiding's court, where Wieland is now living under an assumed name, forging jewellery and weapons for the king. He has fallen in love with Bathilde who now possesses the ring. She, however, conspires with Gram to destroy the smith, whom she alone has recognised. Revealing his true identity to her father, she warns him of Wieland's threatened revenge. The king, who wishes to retain the skilful smith in his service without danger to himself, gives orders to lame Wieland by severing the sinews of his feet.

Act III: Wieland sits at his forge, maimed, brooding over his plight. Bathilde enters and asks him to repair her ring. Wieland recognises the ring, remembers Schwanhilde and curses Bathilde, in whom he sees the cause of all his misfortune. Moved to pity, she tells him that Schwanhilde is not dead: she has seen her flying out to sea from his ruined forge. Wieland, yearning for freedom and reunion with Schwanhilde, forges himself a pair of wings, while the voice of Schwanhilde is heard calling him from on high. At this moment King Neiding enters, followed by his men who mock the lamed smith. Wieland fastens his wings and fans the fire of the forge, which envelops the king and his courtiers. Then he rises into the air to join the swanmaiden. "Schwanhilde floats with wings outspread from the forest to meet him: they join, and fly into the distance."

This dramatic sketch, written for the most part in a rhythmical prose which at times comes close to the metre of the *Ring*, shows some striking affinities to the tetralogy: there is the central function of the ring which gives power (and, in this case, also love) to its owner; there is the sword Wieland forges for the king to ensure his victory in battle. There are many other parallels such as the forging songs the smith sings at his work. The figure of Gram, the king's marshal, has some resemblance to Hagen, while Bathilde is a curious mixture of Ortrud and Brünnhilde. The injured swan, on the other hand, may be seen as an anticipation of the swan episode in *Parsifal*.

However, the plot remains on the level of pure legend, lacking the mythical depth and universal range of the Nibelung drama.

Nevertheless, Wagner's choice of this subject had wider implications than appears at first sight. His personal involvement, his self-identification with the plight of the smith has already been mentioned. The very names are symbolic: *Neiding* (envy) for the king, *Gram* (grief) for his marshal, and others. But there is a yet deeper level of meaning. Wagner placed a poetic rendering of the legend at the end of an essay he wrote at the same time, *Das Kunstwerk der Zukunft (The Work of Art of the Future)*. In this highly charged passage, he identifies the story of Wieland with the struggle of the *Volk* to regain their freedom from oppression, concluding with these challenging words; "Oh unique, glorious *Volk*! This you have created, and you are yourself that Wieland! Forge your wings and soar up high!" (III, 177).

Thus Wagner saw in the *Wieland Saga* a symbol not only of his own ambitions as an artist but of the German *Volk*, both in its revolutionary struggle and as the true creator of myth. It is a key passage, pointing to the very core of the theoretical writings which occupied him during these crucial years.

Wagner offered the draft of *Wieland der Schmied* to the Opéra in Paris, where he had gone from Zürich in a frantic effort to gain a new foothold. His hopes proved as futile as they had been ten years before. Obviously he could hardly have found a subject less suitable to French taste. So this dramatic project, too, came to nothing. In the end it was *Siegfrieds Tod* which remained and from which grew, step by step, *Der Ring des Nibelungen*. But before he could embark on this vast enterprise, he had to clarify his ideas on the interrelation of opera and drama and their integration in a "total work of art".

IV

THE THEORY OF DRAMA

The diversity of dramatic projects which occupied Wagner in the years following the completion of *Lohengrin,* and which—with one exception—all came to nothing, indicates the deep crisis he underwent at this point in his creative development. The political upheaval of 1848–49, which forced him into exile, accentuated this crisis, but it was no more than a contributory factor. He felt that with *Tannhäuser* and *Lohengrin* he had reached the limits of romantic opera in the traditional sense, and that he stood on the threshold of a new art-form the outlines of which he could only dimly perceive. With his urge for self-explanation and self-interpretation he had to state his case theoretically before advancing along this new road.

This he did in the series of prose writings between 1849 and 1852: *Art and Revolution, The Work of Art of the Future,* and finally *Opera and Drama.* Each of these is a stepping-stone to the next; taken together they represent a consistent line of thought, leading from open advocacy of social revolution to the conception of a new art-form. The one cannot be fully understood without the other. But there is a definite logical process: Wagner's active involvement in the political sphere had originated in his dissatisfaction with the operatic world; after the failure of the Revolution he concentrated once more on the purely aesthetic. In other words, his conception of a new art-form combining all the arts evolved directly from his ideas on social revolution. In his preface to these writings in his Collected Works, Wagner himself outlines this development in the following words:"I believed in revolution, as in its necessity and irresistibility ... At the same time, I felt called upon to indicate the road to its salvation. Although it was not my concern to define the new *political* order that was to grow from the debris of a false world, I felt inspired to outline the *work of art* which was to arise from the debris of a false art." (III, 2). Clearly Wagner, at this later date, played down his active involvement in the uprising of 1848, but he was well aware of the process which led him from political to artistic revolution. It is intriguing to follow this process in greater detail.

In the first of his essays, *Die Kunst und die Revolution (Art and Revolution)*, written in the first months of his exile, 1849, Wagner takes as his point of departure a rapturous evocation of the spirit of ancient Greece which found its supreme expression in the *drama*. In glowing words he describes the performance of the great tragedies in the theatre where the people gathered as for a sacred festival: "These people *(Volk)* came together from the state assembly, from the law-courts, from the country, from the ships, from the war camps, from distant regions, filling in their thirty-thousands the amphitheatre, to see the most profound of all tragedies, *Prometheus*, performed, to gather before the most powerful work of art, in order to understand themselves, to comprehend their own activities, to merge into oneness with their being, their fellowship, their god . . ." (III, 11).

With the decline of the Athenian state, tragedy disintegrated into its various components. Philosophy took the place of Art. The Romans, with their realistic and materialistic view of the world, replaced drama with circus spectacles. Christianity, in its turn, with its abnegation of this world and its emphasis on life hereafter, was inimical to Art. When the fervour of religion had burnt itself out, Art became the servant of wordly princes. These were succeeded by the new master of Art—Industry—in other words, by the mercantile spirit of capitalist society. And Wagner proceeds to rail against this spirit and its reflection in the theatre of his time: what is shown there is not "real drama, that one, indivisible, greatest work of art of the human spirit", it is its various components or, generally speaking, its separation into *play* and *opera*. Moreover, the modern theatre serves only the idle entertainment of the rich, in contrast to the theatre of ancient Greece: "In the wide spaces of the Greek amphitheatre, the entire *Volk* attended the performances; in our smart theatres, only its affluent portion is lounging." (III, 20). From this follows a further essential difference: the art of the Greeks was *conservative*, being a valid expression of public consciousness; the genuine art of the present, however, is *revolutionary* since it is in opposition to modern society. In this way, Wagner arrives at the conclusion that only "the great revolution of mankind" can restore Art (that is, drama) to its original wholeness. Only when the slaves of industry have been raised to "free, strong men" will Art be once more the property of all. Thus Art and Revolution must go hand in hand in their struggle for one great goal: "This goal is strong and beautiful Man: may Revolution give him the strength, Art the beauty!" (III, 32).

In the last section of this essay, Wagner touches on more practical matters. He proposes that the theatre, as the most comprehensive and influential artistic institution, should open its doors to the public free of charge. In this way it will become the forerunner and model of all future communal undertakings, preparing the way for a society in which all will be brothers, living a life worthy of man.

It is clear that in this essay Wagner, still under the impact of the 1848 revolution, links his vision of total drama with his demand for violent change in the social order. This link becomes increasingly tenuous in his subsequent essay, *Das Kunstwerk der Zukunft (The Work of Art of the Future)*, 1850.

Wagner starts with a closer definition of what he means by *Volk*—a key-word in his theory of Art: "The *Volk* is the sum total of all those who feel a common need." (III, 48). This *Volk* is the true creator of language, of religion, of the state, of myth. All true Art originates in the *Volk*, whereas its opposites, mannerism and fashion, are artificial stimuli for those who do not feel the common need. Wagner then goes on to examine the basic artistic capacities of man, which in combination have produced the supreme work of art, *drama*.

For drama is born from the union of dance, music, and poetry (in Wagner's terms, *Tanzkunst, Tonkunst,* and *Dichtkunst.*) Each of these arts, taken by itself, is restricted; only in their fusion can man develop all his potentialities freely. Wagner then proceeds to examine the history of each. Dance, left to itself, has degenerated into mime, which tries to present dramatic characters and actions but lacks language. Music, taken singly, has developed to absolute music, which, for want of words to give it meaning, has evolved abstract forms such as counterpoint and the symphony, while folksong has degenerated into the operatic aria. Beethoven's Choral Symphony, with its recourse to words, is both the culmination and turning-point of absolute music. Beyond it no progress is possible; it can be followed only by the art-form Wagner is aiming at all along—the total drama of the future.

Lastly, Poetry: its original, genuine expression was the epic created by the *Volk,* the *Volksepos.* The written epics we know, such as the Homeric epics and the *Nibelungenlied,* are merely literary derivations from these originals. From the latter sprang drama, in which the deeds of the heroes were enacted instead of being merely narrated. Thus drama in its pure form was a creation of the *Volk,* who wished to see their gods and heroes impersonated on the stage. As soon as it ceased to spring from the spirit of the *Volk,* drama declined. It reached another height with Shakespeare, who created his drama "from the innermost nature of the people"—all the more admirable, Wagner adds, as it lives "by the power of speech alone and without the aid of other arts." (III, 109). Thus even Shakespeare is merely a step towards the drama of the future. He stands alone as Beethoven does in music: only when these two "Prometheus"—Shakespeare and Beethoven—join hands, will the future work of art be born.

After Shakespeare, drama degenerated to mere "book drama", that is, it lost its connection with the living stage and became part of literature. Wagner then examines some spurious attempts to reunite the various art-forms. The most obvious is opera. But in opera music dominates, making the other arts subservient to its own laws. Only when the three principal arts, music, poetry, and dance, join and fuse on equal terms, can the true work of art come into being: "The supreme common work of art is drama. It can only exist in its potential fulness when it contains every art-form in its greatest fulness." (III, 150). Even architecture and painting are called upon to serve this consummate purpose. For this drama will require its appropriate theatre where the audience is no longer divided by distinctions of rank and class and the spectator's attention is directed solely to the stage on which the drama is enacted. (Clearly these ideas were largely realised more than twenty years later, in the Bayreuth Festspielhaus.)

But what, Wagner asks, are the conditions which will produce this work of art? His answer is somewhat vaguer than it was in the preceding essay. There is no longer any reference to a social revolution but merely a faint hint that "life" must by itself engender the corresponding art. The only practical suggestion he has to make is an association of all artists cooperating in a common purpose.

Finally, Wagner returns to the theme which was his point of departure—the *Volk* as the creator of all true art. Who, he asks, constitute the *Volk*? Surely not, as some might argue, the "mob" of modern industrial society? For this mob is merely the product of an unnatural civilisation. Only those who, irrespective of class, draw from "true, naked human nature" the strength to revolt against the oppressor, belong to the *Volk*. To illustrate his point, Wagner concludes this essay with a poetic rendering of the *Wieland Saga*, both as an example of genuine folk poetry and as a symbol of revolt. His former revolutionary fervour is reduced to a poetic metaphor.*

The Work of Art of the Future was immediately followed by Wagner's main theoretical work *Oper und Drama (Opera and Drama)* (1851), which is in essence an elaboration of his preceding essay. It consists of three parts: (I) Opera and the

---

* On its first publication in 1850, Wagner preceded this essay by a lengthy dedication to Ludwig Feuerbach in which he acknowledged his indebtedness to the philosopher. This dedication was omitted from the Collected Works.

Nature of Music, (II) Play and the Nature of Dramatic Poetry, (III) Poetry and Music in the Drama of the Future. Since we are here concerned with Wagner as a dramatist, we shall ignore as far as possible those sections dealing exclusively with music.

Wagner opens his survey of operatic history by stating, in block letters, the fundamental fallacy of traditional opera, "that a means of expression (music) has been made the end, the end of expression (drama) the means." (III, 231). He then examines closely the principal components of opera—aria and recitative—and draws the conclusion that in opera the poet is wholly subservient as he shapes the libretto according to the musician's requirements. Even when opera reaches its culmination in Mozart, this relationship is not changed. Had Mozart met a poet congenial to his genius, he might have produced the total drama Wagner has in mind. As it happened, Mozart left the formal structure of opera virtually untouched. After tracing in detail the evolution of Italian, French, and German opera, Wagner arrives at the final verdict that the "madness" of opera consists in the fact that "its means of expression determined the purpose of drama." (III, 308). Music, he argues, is woman who receives the seed from man, dramatic poetry. The union of the two will give birth to the complete work of art.

It is the second part, "Play and the Nature of Dramatic Poetry", which deserves closer attention in the present context. Modern drama, Wagner states apodictically, has a twofold origin—the *novel* and *Greek drama*. This rather puzzling assertion becomes comprehensible when one discovers that for him *novel* comprises epic poems and romances, that is, any narrative art form. The dramatic form closest to narrative was the medieval mystery play, in which entire histories were enacted without selection or compression. The Elizabethan theatre, culminating in Shakespeare, condensed its narrative sources into dramatic action, limiting it in space and time. Racine's *tragédie*, on the other hand, took the opposite road: based on the (misunderstood) rules of Greek drama, it relegated all dramatic action offstage and concentrated on speech as the sole medium of drama.

Between these two extremes, represented by Shakespeare and Racine, dramatic literature has been oscillating ever since.

From this viewpoint, Wagner surveys the history of drama—in particular, of German drama—up to his time. We need not follow his arguments in detail; some of these show brilliant insight, while others are to say the least arbitrary. It must always be borne in mind that he was writing in the mid-nineteenth century when he had only the German classics, above all Goethe and Schiller, and their minor successors to go by. This may account for some of the curious judgments he passes on the literary scene of his own time. Modern drama, he argues, takes its material from the bourgeois novel. This novel has as its object the depiction of present-day life in all its social ramifications, and, by showing up the defects of contemporary society, calls implicitly for its overthrow. In using this material, drama has degenerated to shallow realism—in short, it betrays its true and noble purpose.

Along these lines, Wagner arrives once more at his central idea—drama born from myth, as exemplified by Greek tragedy. "The tragic poet", he concludes, "conveyed the content and essence of myth in the most convincing and intelligible form, and tragedy is nothing but the artistic consummation of myth." (IV, 34). He proceeds to discuss Christian and Germanic myth and their relationship to art. Christian myth, which sees in life merely a preparation for death, is not conducive to the emergence of drama. Germanic myth, on the other hand, being life-affirming like the Greek, created its gods and their human counterparts, heroes, with a wealth of incident and action. (Here, Wagner singles out the *Siegfried Saga,* with an obvious hint at his own prospective work.)

In the third part of *Opera and Drama,* Wagner approaches his goal, the fusion of speech and music in a single work of art, from a new angle. Verbal language, he argues, addresses itself to reason *(Verstand),* whereas the language of music belongs to the realm of feeling *(Gefühl),* of myth, or, in modern terms, the subconscious. "Tonal language is the beginning and end of verbal language, just as feeling is the beginning and end of reason, myth the beginning and end of history . . ." (IV, 91). It is not necessary to enter into the long-winded discussion of the respective properties of music and language, and their relationship to one another. Wagner concludes that neither modern speech nor rhymed nor blank verse are suited to musical treatment but only the alliterative verse *(Stabreim)* of the German language, with its stress on the word-root—in short, the language of the *Ring*.

Finally, Wagner examines the relationship of poet and composer in collaboration. Only if both develop their faculties to the highest level can the perfect drama be achieved. Although the two can well be thought of as separate, they may be united in a single person. In a lengthy footnote, Wagner rejects any suggestion that his argument only serves to propagate his own work. "I am proud", he concludes, "not of my achievements but of what I have understood through them, so that I can now pronounce it with conviction." (IV, 210).

Nevertheless it is obvious that Wagner's whole theoretical edifice, as it unfolds in three successive prose pieces, is in fact directed towards the propagation of his own creative work. It cannot be judged as a valid theory of either drama or opera but as a purely subjective conception, intended to clarify for himself and for others what he was aiming at as an artist. His theoretical writings would long be forgotten, had they not been realised in the works of his maturity, above all in the gigantic work that was growing in his mind—*Der Ring des Nibelungen*. As soon as he returned to creative work, he abandoned all theorising. In his later years, he even professed an aversion to "the labyrinth of theoretical speculation". In one of the few larger essays, *Zukunftsmusik (Music of the Future)*, of 1860 (written for a French friend in preparation for the Paris performance of *Tannhäuser*), he calls the conditions under which he wrote these essays "an abnormal state such as may occur once in the life of an artist but cannot well be repeated." (VII, 88). For the rest of his life his numerous prose writings consisted mainly of comparatively short articles written on specific occasions and subjects.

It is worth noting that in all his theoretical writings Wagner never uses the term "music drama" but always speaks of "drama". In *A Communication to my Friends*, written shortly after the completion of *Opera and Drama*, he states explicitly: "I don't write operas any longer: as I do not wish to invent an arbitrary name for my works, I call them *dramas,* because this denotes most clearly the point of view from which what I offer should be received." (IV, 343).

It must, however, be borne in mind that his conception of drama includes music as an integral part. In a special article, *Uber die Benennung "Musikdrama" (On the Designation "Music Drama")* of 1872, the year the foundation stone of the Bayreuth Festspielhaus was laid, he firmly rejects, on linguistic grounds, the term which had meanwhile come into use. In its stead he chooses the name *Bühnenfestspiel* (stage festival play), which emphasises the "stage play" as the most distinctive aspect of the work he was about to present.

V

WORLD MYTH:
DER RING DES NIBELUNGEN

In its conception and range of vision *Der Ring des Nibelungen (The Ring of the Nibelung)* is undoubtedly Wagner's greatest work (though not necessarily his most perfect). No other work of his has called forth so many commentaries and interpretations, from Shaw's socio-economic interpretation in *The Perfect Wagnerite* of 1898 to Robert Donington's Jungian analysis, *Wagner's 'Ring' and its Symbols*, of 1963. No doubt many more will follow. Each views the work from a particular and indeed often from an idiosyncratic angle. This variety of approaches only proves that the *Ring*—like all great works of art—moves on many levels, any one of which reveals itself at a different historical moment.

I have no intention of offering yet another interpretation of the *Ring*. What I mean to do is to trace its genesis from its first conception in 1848 to the completion of the text in 1852, and to appraise the work in purely dramatic terms.

The vast project of the *Ring* tetralogy grew, as has been shown, from a deep crisis in Wagner's evolution as an artist. In turning to this project, he writes in *A Communication*, "I had entered a new and decisive period of my artistic and human development: the period of *conscious artistic will* on an entirely new . . . road, on which I am now walking, as an artist and a man, towards a new world." (IV, 320). What is the essence of this new world? Not only did he turn his back on the combination of history and legend which had character-ised his previous works, he also abandoned the auto-biographical element, that is, the self-portrayal as a solitary figure in conflict with the world, which is the key-note of *Der fliegende Holländer*, *Tannhäuser* and *Lohengrin*. Instead, the idea of a drama based on popular myth was as it were an objective conception, in which autobiographical elements had no place. Wagner felt himself to be the mouthpiece of the *Volk* who had created that myth, and it was the *Volk* to whom his work was addressed.

Ever since his first return from Paris, when he immersed himself in the German past, he was attracted to the world of medieval legend. This attraction was deepened by his study of Jacob Grimm's *German Mythology* and similar books. For the next few years his interest centred on medieval history and legend, leading to *Tannhäuser* and *Lohengrin*. Gradually, however, his studies carried him further back to the primary sources of Nordic myth. When the figure of Siegfried superseded the Emperor Barbarossa, it was not the Siegfried of the German *Nibelungenlied* but of the Icelandic *Edda* and its associated sagas. Wagner describes this process in retrospect: "Although the glorious figure of Siegfried had attracted me for a long time, it enchanted me fully only when I had succeeded in seeing it in its purest human manifestation, freed from all later disguises. Only now did I realise the possibility of making him the hero of a drama, which would have never occurred to me as long as I knew him only from the medieval *Nibelungenlied*." (IV, 312).

The sources from which Wagner drew his dramatic cycle need not be traced here in detail.* They are, in the first place, the *Volsunga Saga* and the *Edda*, both written in the early 13th century but based on oral traditions reaching much further back. While the *Volsunga Saga* tells mainly the story of the Volsungs, descendants of Odin, the *Edda* is composed of a multitude of separate sagas, recounting the building of Valhalla, the prophecy of the end of the world, and the story of Sigurd and his treacherous murder by Hogni. All these strands Wagner has ingeniously woven into one continuous

* Wolfgang Golther has listed Fouqué, Uhland, Simrock, Mone, Lachmann, Wilhelm Grimm, Müller, von der Hagen, Jacob Grimm and translations of the *Edda* by Ettmüller and Simrock. (For details, see Bibliography.)

action, stretching from the rape of the Rhinegold to its return to the riverbed.

It is a well-known fact that the *Ring* tetralogy was written backwards, that is, starting from the end and working back to the beginning. The various stages of this creative process are a fascinating subject for closer study.

The first extensive reference to the Nibelung myth occurs in the essay *Die Wibelungen* of 1848. Here Wagner traces the figure of Siegfried back to its mythical origin in the light and sun god, his slaying of the dragon symbolising the triumph of day over night. By winning the gold from the Nibelungs, the children of night and death, he attains immeasurable power. But the dragon's heir kills him treacherously, as night kills day, and drags him down into the dark realm of death. Here is clearly the core of the myth on which Wagner based his work.

This essay was immediately followed by *Der Nibelungen-Mythus (The Nibelung Myth)* designated as "Draft of a Drama", which contains, in a continuous narrative, the action of the whole cycle. Wagner begins by establishing the three races which share the world between them—Nibelungs, giants, and gods: "From the womb of night and death there was born a race which inhabits Nibelheim, i.e. subterranean clefts and caves: they are called *Nibelungen*; with restless activity they burrow (like worms in a dead body) through the entrails of the earth: they heat, purify, and forge the hard metals." (II, 156). One of them, Alberich, seizes the Rhinegold, forges from it a ring that gives him power over his fellow dwarves, and the tarnhelm through which he can change his shape at will. Thus equipped, he aspires to rule the world. The giants, on the other hand, uncouth and dimwitted, watch with anxiety Alberich's schemes, unable to pit their physical strength against his cunning. Above these two races dwell the gods, who rule the world by law. With their aid the giants gain possession of the ring, but, too stupid to use its power, entrust it to a dragon to guard. Through breaking their self-set laws the gods have become guilty. Only "a free will, independent of the gods" can redeem them. To this purpose, the gods raise up man to act by his own free will. Eventually, the sought-for hero is born from

arther details of how he
ow he was tricked by the
he dragon and gained
ts powers. Lastly, in Act
mpanions the story of his
the final version, except
e: for whereas in *Götter-*
c love, here he visualises
d him to Valhalla—an
g of the drama.

st widely from the version
rds, before she mounts the

in Wort!
ich auf:
ch Rührige band,–
empfah'n,–

e:
her du!
len!
h dir zu:
hen Gruss,
er Macht!

rds!
nd of your bondage:
bound you
gain
you!

rule:
rious one!
pes!
gfried to thee:
h loving welcome
eternal power!)

Das Rheingold: Alberich and the Rhine maidens,
by Knut Ekwall, 1876.

the race of the Wälsungs—Siegmund. Th[e]
corresponds roughly to the later tetra[
essential difference: at the end Brünnhilde l[e]
to Valhalla, which shines in renewed splend[
immolation she has purged the guilt of the
rule supreme.

So the drama, as Wagner first conceived it
an optimistic note, with the rule of the gods [
can be little doubt that this conception
revolutionary ideas which filled him at the t[
Nibelungs representing the toiling industrial p[
giants the "unproductive" propertied class, w[
finally establish the Utopia of a society freed fro[
they hope to achieve through man, represented
heroes, Siegmund and Siegfried. These ideas s[
basis of the final work, though they are overlaid b[
refuted by the pessimistic ending—the doom o[f

The story, as told by Wagner in *Der Nibelung[*
shows a distinct evolution: starting with gods, [
dwarves, that is, with mythological, superhuman
ends on a purely human plane. This evolu[
distinguishes the four successive dramas of the
Rheingold (The Rhinegold) is enacted by eleme[
mythical characters only, *Die Walküre (The Valk[*
Siegfried by a mixture of superhuman and human
while *Götterdämmerung (The Twilight of the Gods)*
almost entirely to the world of men.

One fact stands out in the original draft: the conten[
first three dramas together take up only about half th[
given to the fourth, which is told with a wealth of det[
even some dialogue. Clearly it was Wagner's o[
intention to write an opera on the death of Siegfried [
would contain, like Greek tragedy, only the final catastr[
gradually revealing the events that had brought it about.
is precisely what he did in *Siegfrieds Tod (Siegfried's De[*
designated as "A grand heroic opera", which he w[
immediately after *Der Nibelungen-Mythus*, in the autum[
1848, while still in Dresden.

The action of *Siegfrieds Tod* corresponds—with so[

latter imparts to his sleeping son f[
seized the gold and forged the ring, [
gods, and how Siegfried slew [
possession of the ring, unaware of [
III, Siegfried tells his hunting co[
life—a scene largely unchanged in [
for his dying words to Brünnhild[
dämmerung he recalls their ecstati[
her as a Valkyrie ready to le[
anticipation of the different endi[

It is this ending which differs m[
we know. Brünnhilde's closing wo[
funeral pyre, are as follows;

Ihr Nibelungen, vernehmt me[
eure Knechtschaft künd[
der den Ring geschmiedet, eu[
nicht soll er ihn wieder [
doch frei sei er, wie ihr[

. . . Nur einer herrsch[
Allvater! Herrli[
Freu' dich des freiesten Hel[
Siegfried führ' i[
biet' ihm minnli[
dem Bürgen ewi[

(Ye Nibelungs, hear my wo[
I announce the [
he who forged the ring and[
shall not get it [
but be free like[

. . . Only one shall[
All-father! Glo[
Rejoice in the freest of her[
I shall lead Sie[
Receive him w[
who ensures th[

As she mounts the pyre, a chorus of men and women (omitted in the final version) extol her and Siegfried. Finally we see Brünnhilde, once again a Valkyrie, taking Siegfried's body to Valhalla.

So there is no question of an end to the gods. Freed from guilt, their power will last for ever. The Nibelungs, too, are set free, and Brünnhilde is restored to her divine status. Thus this first version corresponds to Wagner's original idea as laid down in his prose sketch *Der Nibelungen-Mythus*: the gods elect a free man to exculpate them from their guilt and restore them to their former glory. That man is Siegfried. The complex story leading up to his drama is reduced to a minimum: Wotan, who stands at the centre of the final tetralogy, is barely mentioned, nor are Siegmund and Sieglinde and the story of their tragic love. Despite these reductions, the events preceding Siegfried's drama are bound to remain all but unintelligible: there is a distinct rift between the myth of the gods and the essentially human tragedy of Siegfried's death, indicative of the two separate sagas Wagner tried to weld together.

Wagner was well aware of this unsatisfactory solution—it may be one of the reasons why he abandoned, for the time being, the plan for a Siegfried opera and turned to other projects, *Jesus von Nazareth* and *Wieland der Schmied*. He returned to it only in the spring of 1851, as an exile in Zürich. Liszt, who had brought out the first performance of *Lohengrin* in Weimar, asked Wagner to let him have a new work, suggesting *Siegfrieds Tod*. However, when Wagner set out to sketch the music to his text he realised the impossibility of composing it as an isolated work. So he conceived the plan of *Der junge Siegfried* to precede it as "a heroic comedy". In a letter to his friend Uhlig he wrote: "Haven't I written to you once before about a cheerful subject? It was the lad who sets out 'to learn fear', and is too stupid to learn it. Imagine my shock when I suddenly realised that the lad is none other than—young Siegfried, who wins the treasure and wakes Brünnhilde!" (Wagner/ Uhlig, 91). Inspired by the spring and "in the best mood", he completed the text within three weeks.

Die Walküre: the death of Siegmund, by Knut Ekwall, 1876.

Der junge Siegfried* is practically identical with the final *Siegfried,* except for a few minor divergencies: Wotan appears still as Wodan; Siegfried's sword is still called Balmung, not Notung; in Act I, Siegfried chases successively two wild beasts, a wolf and a bear, into Mime's dwelling, not just a bear. But there are two differences of some interest: in Act III, Wotan does not bar Siegfried's way with his spear and Siegfried does not shatter it—a crucial turning point in the final version. And in the Brünnhilde-Siegfried scene at the end, Brünnhilde has a long narration in which she tells the story of the Wälsungs, the incestuous love of Siegmund and Sieglinde, her own disobedience to Wotan, and her punishment. This account was obviously redundant after *Die Walküre* was written. But there is one point of major importance: evidently Wagner had conceived, since completing *Siegfrieds Tod,* a different ending to the whole drama. For in the great scene between Wotan and Erda-Wala, the latter prophesies the end of the gods—and Wotan accepts it by his own free will:

> *Der Götter Ende*
> *erkenn' auch ich:*
> *doch es sorgt mich nicht*
> *seit ich es* will!
>
> (*The end of the gods*
> *I, too, foresee:*
> *but it troubles me not*
> *since I have willed it!*)

So now there were two Siegfried dramas, one a "heroic comedy" and one a tragedy. And Wagner promised Liszt that he would set *Der junge Siegfried* to music at once, believing it was the easier of the two to compose. However, something kept him from starting work. A few months later, in November 1851, he suddenly drafted in quick succession a prose sketch of a "Prelude", *Das Rheingold* (first called *Der*

* *Der junge Siegfried* was first published complete in *Skizzen und Entwürfe zur Ring-Dichtung,* ed. by Otto Strobel, Munich, 1930.

Raub des Rheingoldes or *The Rape of the Rhinegold*) and of the first two acts of *Die Walküre*, with Wotan still appearing in person in Hunding's house to thrust the sword into the tree-trunk. Wagner described the whole creative process in a long letter to Liszt, explaining why he could let him have neither *Siegfrieds Tod* nor *Der junge Siegfried:*

"In the autumn of 1848 I first drafted the complete myth of the Nibelungs as it now belongs to me as my poetic property. My next attempt at dramatising the main catastrophe of the great action for our theatre was *Siegfried's Death*. After hesitating for a long time, I was at last, in the autumn of 1850, about to draft the musical composition of that drama when the impossibility of having it anywhere satisfactorily performed deflected me from this task. To rid myself of this desperate mood, I wrote the book *Opera and Drama*. But *Siegfried's Death* was, I knew, for the time being impossible. I realised that first I had to prepare for it by another drama, and so I took up a plan I had cherished for some time, of making *Young Siegfried* the subject of a poem; in it everything that was partly narrated, partly taken for granted in *Siegfried's Death,* was to be actually represented, in fresh, vivid outline. This poem was quickly drafted and completed ... This *Young Siegfried*, too, is only a fragment ... In these two dramas a number of necessary references were left solely to narration or even to the guesswork of the audience . . . I must therefore convey my entire myth, in its deepest and widest significance, with artistic distinctness, in order to be fully understood. Nothing of it must in any way be left to be filled in by thought or by reflection; any simple human sensibility must be able, with its organs of artistic perception, to conceive *the whole,* because only then can it properly understand every single part. So two principal motives of my myth are left for me to present, and both of them are suggested in *Young Siegfried* ..." He then describes in vivid terms the contents of *Die Walküre* and goes on: "Think of this wealth of stimulation for a drama preceding the two Siegfrieds, and you will understand that it was no mere reflection but rather enthusiasm that inspired my latest plan!

Siegfried: Brünnhilde's awakening, by Knut Ekwall. 1876.

"This plan now aims at three dramas: 1. *The Valkyrie*, 2. *Young Siegfried*, 3. *Siegfried's Death*. However, in order to represent everything completely, these three dramas must be preceded by a great prelude: *The Rape of the Rhinegold*. Its subject is the complete representation of all that occurs in *Young Siegfried* in the form of narration, relating to that rape, the origin of the Nibelungs' hoard, the capture of this hoard by Wotan, and Alberich's curse."

Wagner concludes this revealing letter by outlining the way he visualises his huge cycle to be staged: "The performance of my Nibelung dramas must take place at a great festival, organised perhaps for the specific purposes of the performance. It must take place on three successive days, with the introductory prelude given the night before." (Wagner/Liszt, I, 145 ff). It was to take twenty-five years for this dream to come true!

After producing further, more detailed, prose drafts of the two remaining pieces, Wagner completed the full texts in 1852 —first of *Die Walküre*, then of *Das Rheingold*. So the whole cycle was in fact written backwards. Then he turned to revising the two other dramas, which had to be brought into line with the whole cycle. To start with, many narrative passages could now be eliminated or curtailed since their contents were visibly enacted in the first two dramas. This applied in particular to Wotan's encounter with Alberich at the beginning of Act II of *Der junge Siegfried*, to Brünnhilde's long narration after her awakening, and to Alberich's explanations to the sleeping Hagen in *Siegfrieds Tod*. It might be argued that Wagner didn't go far enough: there are undoubtedly several passages which seem dramatically redundant as they merely reiterate what we know already, such as Wotan's lengthy narration to Brünnhilde in *Die Walküre*, Act II, or the exchange of the all too obvious riddles between Wotan and Mime, both of which have lost their original function of informing the audience of relevant facts. Others, however, are too fully integrated into the action (not to speak of their musical value) to be considered expendable—as, for instance, Siegfried's recapitulation of his youth just before his death. In such narrative passages, Wagner's basic problem of transforming epic into drama has left its traces.

More important than any excisions, however, are the actual changes Wagner undertook. For the centre of gravity had now shifted from Siegfried, the hero of the last two dramas, to Wotan, who now visibly or invisibly, had come to dominate the whole tetralogy. Moreover, the original ending with the gods restored to their power was replaced by one depicting their doom, symbolised by the burning of Valhalla. This entailed an incisive revision of some key scenes, especially in the final drama, *Siegfrieds Tod*, later renamed *Götterdämmerung (The Twilight of the Gods)*. First of all, the opening scene of the Norns was completely rewritten. Originally, the three sisters while weaving their rope had told each other of the theft of the Rhinegold, the building of Valhalla, and so on. Now they cast their thoughts further back to the very beginning of time: they talk of the world-ash which holds up the universe (the Yggdrasil of the *Edda*). Once upon a time Wotan had broken a branch from its stem and cut the shaft of his spear from it. By this act he violated the primal harmony of Nature: ever since the ashtree has withered away. When Siegfried shatters the spear, Wotan orders the dead ashtree to be felled and its fragments piled around Valhalla ready to be set alight by Loge's fire. As one of the Norns asks when this will happen, their rope becomes entangled and finally snaps. With the cry *Es riss!* (It breaks!) the three sisters descend to their mother, Wala, the earth-goddess. This important scene, rarely understood in its full implications, sets the stage for the whole tragedy as Wagner finally conceived it. Similarly, the original scene between Brünnhilde and the Valkyries is supplanted by the scene between Brünnhilde and Waltraute, in which the latter gives her moving account of Wotan seated on his throne, the broken spear in his hand, silently awaiting the end.

But the most significant change occurs at the end of the whole cycle: instead of Brünnhilde taking Siegfried's body to Valhalla, she hurls a torch onto the pyre with the words:

> *Denn der Götter Ende*
> *dämmert nun auf:*
> *So—werf' ich den Brand*
> *in Walhalls prangende Burg.*

(For the end of the gods
is darkening now:
Thus—I throw the brand
Into Valhalla's shining hall.)

So the whole drama, instead of revolving around Siegfried, the hero who by his deeds and death secures the lasting power of the gods, centres on the deeds of Wotan. The original revolutionary activist conception is transformed into a Passion.

After completing the tetralogy, Wagner had it printed, in 1853, in a small private edition.* He also read the whole work on four successive evenings to a circle of friends in Zürich.

But this was not yet the end of the text to the *Ring*. In the autumn of 1854, Wagner read a book which had a decisive influence on his intellectual development—Schopenhauer's *The World as Will and Idea*. In his autobiography *My Life*, Wagner devotes several pages to Schopenhauer and the impact his work made on him. What impressed him was not so much the aesthetics of music as the metaphysics "because here the negation of the will and complete renunciation are shown to be the only true and ultimate salvation *(Erlösung)* from individual limitation in the conception of and encounter with the world." (XV, 82). Wagner was fully aware that this philosophy was diametrically opposed to the ideas of social and political liberation—in other words, the ideas of Feuerbach and Bakunin—he had held before. But the profound pessimism of Schopenhauer's philosophy, its demonstration of the vanity and futility of life, was in keeping with Wagner's mood, as it was with the mood of the post-revolutionary era. Moreover, Wagner felt that in his creative work he had already subconsciously anticipated Schopenhauer's ideas before encountering them. "I looked at my poem of the Nibelungs and realised to my astonishment that what captivated me in theory had long since been familiar to me in my own poetic conception. Thus I myself understood only now my Wotan and returned deeply moved to a closer

---

* The first public edition appeared only in 1863, with the two last dramas under their definitive names, *Siegfried* and *Götterdämmerung*.

study of Schopenhauer's book . . . From now on the book never entirely left me for many years . . . Its gradual effect on me was extraordinary and decisive for my whole life." As a token of his reverence, he sent a copy of the *Ring* to Schopenhauer, who, though he never acknowledged its receipt, is said to have commented: "The fellow is a poet and not a musician!"

Wagner's belief that in the *Ring* he had anticipated Schopenhauer's ideas before actually encountering them is vividly expressed in a letter he wrote to his friend Röckel (August 23, 1856): "I hardly noticed that in the execution, indeed already in the drafting of the plan, I had subconsciously followed quite a different, much deeper conception, and that I had visualised, instead of a phase in the world's development, the very essence of the world in all its conceivable phases, and had recognised its futility; as I remained faithful to my conception and not to my abstract concepts, of course something very different ensued from what I had actually imagined." (Wagner/Röckel, 67).

Under the impact of Schopenhauer, Wagner wrote a further version of Brünnhilde's closing words in *Götterdämmerung* (the third or, taking into account some minor variants, the fifth), which he included in the final publication though he never set them to music:

> Führ' ich nun nicht mehr
> nach Walhalls Feste,
> wisst ihr, wohin ich fahre?
> Aus Wunschheim zieh' ich fort,
> Wahnheim flieh' ich auf immer;
> des ew'gen Werdens
> off'ne Tore
> schliess' ich hinter mir zu:
> nach dem wunsch-und wahnlos
> heiligsten Wahlland,
> der Welt-Wanderung Ziel,
> von Wiedergeburt erlöst,
> zieht nun die Wissende hin.
> Alles Ew'gen

> *sel'ges Ende,*
> *wisst ihr, wie ichs gewann?*
> *Trauernder Liebe*
> *tiefstes Leiden*
> *schloss die Augen mir auf:*
> *enden sah ich die Welt.*

> *(If I no longer*
> *go to Valhalla*
> *do you know where I go?*
> *From the land of desire I depart,*
> *from the land of illusion for ever I flee;*
> *the open gates*
> *of eternal change*
> *I close behind me:*
> *to the hallowed chosen land*
> *without desire and illusion*
> *the end of world's wandering*
> *delivered from rebirth*
> *with full knowledge I go.*
> *The blissful end*
> *of all eternity*
> *do you know how I attained it?*
> *Deepest suffering*
> *of sorrowing love*
> *has opened my eyes:*
> *I saw the world end.)*

These verses, steeped in Schopenhauer's philosophy and actually using some of his key-terms, hardly seem to belong to the *Ring* any longer; they point ahead to *Tristan* and *Parsifal*. In fact, shortly after reading *The World as Will and Idea*, in the autumn of 1854, Wagner conceived the plan of *Tristan und Isolde*, in which Parsifal was to meet the mortally wounded Tristan.

What is most striking, in contemplating the *Ring* as a whole, is the sheer dramatic skill with which Wagner has organised the diverse epic material on which he has drawn, condensing it into a continuous and consistent action. To start with the dramatic structure: each of the three main dramas is in three acts—the form he had adopted since *Der fliegende Holländer* and retained to the end; only *Das Rheingold*, expressly designated a "prelude", is in four continuous scenes. The entire cycle is carried, on the model of Greek drama, by a comparatively small number of characters. More astonishing, these characters—gods, giants, dwarves, heroes, in short, creations of primordial mythology—touch our deepest emotions, and this not only through the power of the music, but through their humanised passions and conflicts which are the essence of drama. And all this couched in a language which, though admittedly liable to occasional infelicities and crudities, is always to the point and often rises to heights of genuine poetry.

The *Ring* tetralogy looked at as a whole represents no less than a universal world myth. At its beginning and end is pure, timeless Nature—the flowing waters of the Rhine, with their elemental inhabitants, the Rhine maidens, playing around the innocent gold, hailing the light of the sun. Between these two ageless states, the whole drama of the world runs its course, enacted by the gods, their counterparts, the dark creatures of the nether world, and the human race. The two motive forces of this drama are Power and Love: the conflict between these two is at the root of the entire action.

At the beginning, the world is inhabited only by superhuman and subhuman beings—the gods on the heights, headed by Wotan, and the subterranean Nibelungs, headed by Alberich. Both of them aspire to world domination, but each does so on different terms: Alberich, by stealing the gold from which he forges the ring, the symbol of power, and by renouncing love, strives to govern the world by brute force; Wotan, on the other hand, aims at ruling by laws, engraved in runes on the shaft of his spear. The clash between these two mutually exclusive ambitions constitutes the basic conflict pervading the whole drama, from which all other conflicts derive. Both Wotan and Alberich have violated the innocent state of Nature—Alberich by snatching the gold from the depths, Wotan by cutting his spear from the world-ash. Moreover, by forcibly taking the ring from Alberich to pay the giants who have built Valhalla, Wotan breaks his self-imposed rules—world dominion by law—and thus becomes guilty. In fact, his guilt is greater than Alberich's, as the latter cleverly argues when Wotan is about to take his ring:

> *Hüte dich,*
> *herrischer Gott!*
> *Frevelte ich,*
> *so frevelt' ich frei an mir:*
> *doch an allem, was war,*
> *ist und wird,*
> *frevelst, Ewiger, du,*
> *entreissest du frech mir den Ring!*

> *(Beware, imperious god!*
> *If I have trespassed*
> *I have freely sinned against myself:*
> *but you, eternal god,*
> *sin against all that was,*
> *is and shall be,*
> *if you snatch the ring from me!)*

This guilt of Wotan, in which he gets more and more entangled as the action unfolds, drives him to withdraw from the world he had hoped to rule and to create a free man who (as he explains to Fricka), "free from divine protection, rids himself of the law of the gods". This free man is, first, Siegmund, then Siegfried. Both fail, though for different reasons: Siegmund is struck down by the hand of Wotan himself, compelled by Fricka to uphold the moral law of marriage, while Siegfried falls victim to the plots of Hagen, Alberich's son.

The tragedies of Siegmund and Siegfried, the successive protagonists of the three main dramas of the *Ring*, are closely linked to that of Wotan, but they touch us by their own intrinsic pathos. Of the two, Siegmund's tragedy is the more immediately affecting as it unfolds within a single drama—more precisely, within two acts. In the *Volsunga Saga*, on which Wagner largely based his story, Siegmund is the son of Volsa, who in turn is Odin's son. Wagner has foreshortened this relationship by making Siegmund the child of Wotan, who, in the human guise of Wälse, brings him up hunting and fighting at his side. One day he vanishes, leaving only a wolf's skin behind. (Siegmund's allusions to *Wölfe* and *Wölfing* derive from the saga according to which the Volsung clan roam the land as were-wolves, outlaws from human society.) Siegmund shares the fate of the Wälsungs: he feels himself an outcast, shunned by his fellow-men, harassed by misfortune. He, too, is an outsider, in conflict with established rules, kindred to the Flying Dutchman and Tannhäuser. He, too, gains the love of a woman in the face of social convention. The triangle Dutchman-Senta-Erik is repeated in the triangle Siegmund-Sieglinde-Hunding. It will recur, on a higher plane, in the constellation Tristan-Isolde-Marke. Always it is the romantic outsider who breaks into an established relationship and carries off the woman by the overriding claim of passion. Siegmund's case is aggravated by the fact that she is his own sister. Because of this two-fold offence against the moral law—adultery and incest—Wotan is forced, at Fricka's bidding, to kill his own son, and break the sword he himself has given him. This sword is the third material symbol of the whole cycle, next to Alberich's ring, the symbol of unlimited power, and Wotan's spear, the symbol of rule by law.

Wotan's first attempt to let a free man, unrestrained by laws, win the world for him has failed. He is forced, against his will, not only to desert his son but also to punish Brünnhilde, his favourite daughter, for wanting to carry out what was his original intention. This is in fact the culminating point of his tragedy, as he expresses it in his desperate outburst to Brünnhilde in the second act of *Die Walküre*:

> *Ich berührte Alberichs Ring—*
> *gierig hielt ich das Gold!*
> > *Der Fluch, den ich floh,*
> > *nicht flieht er nun mich:–*
> *was ich liebe, muss ich verlassen,*
> *morden, was je ich minne,*

> *trügend verraten,*
> *wer mir vertraut!–*

> *. . . Zusammen breche,*
> *was ich gebaut!*
> *Auf geb' ich mein Werk;*
> *eines nur will ich noch:*
> *das Ende—das Ende!*

> *(I touched Alberich's ring–*
> *greedily I held the gold!*
> *The curse I evaded*
> *does not evade me:*
> *I must leave what I love,*
> *murder whoever I cherish,*
> *deceive and betray*
> *whoever trusts me!–*

> *. . . What I have built*
> *let it fall in ruins!*
> *I give up my work;*
> *one thing only I will:*
> *the end—the end!)*

From this moment, Wotan *wills* the end Erda has foretold. He resigns his divine power and roams the world only as a Wanderer, a passive onlooker.

However, Brünnhilde, by saving Sieglinde and the fragments of the sword, gives Wotan a second chance—Siegfried. His tragedy extends over two dramas, *Siegfried* and *Götterdämmerung*. He is the precise opposite of Siegmund: ignorant of his descent, carefree and untroubled by any past, brought up amidst the birds and beasts of the forest, he is a child of nature. One could say that the two heroes, in Wagner's hands, represent two contrasting archetypes of the Romantic imagination: the one the ill-fated outcast, doomed from the outset by a curse overhanging him, the other the guileless simpleton of fairy-tale. This contrast is reflected in their natural surroundings: while Siegmund's first entrance is accompanied by the raging storm, Siegfried is imaged

Götterdämmerung: the dead Siegfried, by Knut Ekwall, 1876.

stretched out under the lindentree conversing with the birds of the forest. Thus it is Siegfried, rather than Siegmund, who seems predestined to fulfil Wotan's great scheme. Unlike Siegmund, who has been given the sword by Wotan, he forges it anew by his own effort. Fearlessly, he kills the dragon and passes through the fire surrounding Brünnhilde's rock. His union with Brünnhilde is unclouded by any guilt; it is an ecstatic affirmation of life which laughs even at death: *Leuchtende Liebe! Lachender Tod!* (Radiant love! Smiling death!) In short, he is truly the free man Wotan has envisaged. When the two meet at the foot of the rock, it is now his sword which shatters Wotan's spear—the last and decisive turning-point in the god's decline from power. Wotan's words to Siegfried as he picks up the pieces of his spear, "Go hence! I cannot hold you!" are the last we hear from his lips. After that, he retires to Valhalla, round which he has piled the logs from the world-ash, wordlessly awaiting the end.

Siegfried's tragedy, which is the main subject of *Götter-dämmerung*, results not from any offence of his own but from the machinations of his dark foe, Hagen, the son of Alberich. In the confrontation Siegfried-Hagen the cosmic struggle between Wotan and Alberich—the basic theme of the whole cycle—is carried on. For Hagen is merely instrumental to Alberich's scheme for regaining the ring, now on Siegfried's finger. The means by which he tries to attain his ends—the potion of oblivion—is, as has often been pointed out, one of the weaker links in Wagner's plot (unlike the love potion in *Tristan*, which is fully justified psychologically). Through this potion Siegfried turns traitor without knowing it and thus brings about his own death. But Hagen's plan misfires: Brünnhilde, finally aware of Siegfried's innocence, takes the ring back as she mounts the funeral pyre, bequeathing it to the Rhine maidens. Thus the ring, which has brought nothing but strife and death on its way through the world, returns to the elements whence its gold has been taken at the beginning. The cycle is closed and the state of guiltless Nature restored. Valhalla goes up in flames. Is it only the end of the gods or the end of the world, as in the Ragnorok of the *Edda*? The key to this question is contained, if anywhere, in Brünnhilde's closing words. It is significant that Wagner has supplied several variants of these words, from the optimistic ending of the first version to the Schopenhauerian pessimism of the last, which concludes with the line: *Enden sah ich die Welt* (I have seen the world end). Ultimately, it is in the music that we must look for an answer: after the shattering chords signifying the burning of Valhalla, there rises the great theme generally known as "redemption through love". The meaning is clear: the world, purged from the curse of the ring, is redeemed by love triumphant in Brünnhilde's self-immolation. In other words, the idea of redemption, Wagner's basic theme, is here applied not to an individual, but to the world as a whole.

VI

LOVE AND DEATH:
TRISTAN UND ISOLDE

Wagner first conceived the idea of *Tristan und Isolde* in 1854. However, for the time being he put it aside as he was fully occupied with the composition of the *Ring*. In the following year another subject began to attract him, a Buddhist legend, *Die Sieger (The Victors)*. His immersion in Schopenhauer had led him to the related ideas of Buddhism. In Burnouf's *Introduction à l'histoire de buddhisme indien* he found a story which impressed him deeply: it concerns a girl from the low Chandala caste who falls in love with one of Buddha's disciples. In a former life, which lies open to the allknowing Buddha, she had been a wealthy girl who had scorned the love of a wooer. Under the influence of Buddha's teachings she renounces her love and is finally accepted into his order. What fascinated Wagner in this story was the interplay of past and present or, as he puts it, the "double life" of the principal characters, which offered ample opportunities for his new musical technique of thematic allusions and cross-references.

Of this project, only a short prose sketch of 1856 survives, giving an outline of the action. Parcriti—later renamed Savitri—a humble Chandala girl, meets Buddha's favourite disciple, Ananda, at a well and falls passionately in love with him. She approaches Buddha, who is resting at the town gate, and begs to be united with Ananda. Buddha consents on condition that she joins in his disciple's vow of chastity. He knows of her former incarnation as a wealthy Brahmin's daughter, who had haughtily rejected the love of a prince. As a punishment, she has been reborn into her present low caste and now has to suffer the pangs of unrequited love. Only through renunciation can she be redeemed and received into the community of Buddha. The girl joyfully accepts this condition and is welcomed by Ananda as a sister. The draft closes with the words: "Buddha's last teachings. All profess his religion. He wanders towards the place of his deliverance *(Erlösung)*."

Evidently, this story, centring on a painful conflict between passion and renunciation, deeply affected Wagner, who at the time was struggling against his growing involvement with Mathilde Wesendonck. Two years later, in a long passage of his Venetian diary written for Mathilde, he returns once more to the subject, elaborating his thoughts on Buddha and his doctrine of deliverance from the world's sufferings. He sees himself and Mathilde as Ananda and Savitri, happy in their renunciation.

The project of *Die Sieger* never matured. Its essence was absorbed in *Parsifal*: Savitri was transformed into Kundry, who abjures her sensual love under the purifying influence of the Grail-knight. But the idea of *Die Sieger* never quite left Wagner's mind: even after the completion of *Parsifal*, in the last year of his life, he returned to it once more, and it is said that he was occupied with the Buddhist legend at the time of his death.

For some time *Die Sieger* and *Tristan* competed in Wagner's mind; in the end *Tristan* prevailed. The contrast between the drama of renunciation and that of consummate fulfilment is not as irreconcilable as appears at first sight. In the first conception of *Tristan und Isolde* in 1854, the wounded knight was to be visited in the last act by Parsifal on his way to the Grail. Moreover, the figure of Tristan, longing for death yet unable to die, merged, as Wagner writes, with that of Amfortas. This plan was presently dropped, or rather it split into two separate works.

In December 1854 Wagner wrote in a letter to Liszt: "Since I have never in my life tasted the real happiness of love, I shall raise a monument to this most beautiful of all dreams, in which from beginning to end that love will be thoroughly satiated. I have drafted in my mind a *Tristan and Isolde*, the simplest but most fullblooded musical conception; with the 'black flag' that waves at the end, I shall cover myself to die." (Wagner/Liszt, II, 46).

There was to be no black flag in the final version, but the fusion of love and death, the quintessence of the drama, was there from the outset. It was, as Wagner writes, the "serious mood into which Schopenhauer had put me, and which strove for an ecstatic expression of its basic features", (XV, 83) which suggested to him the drama of *Tristan und Isolde*.

Another three years elapsed before Wagner returned to the project, completing the text in the summer of 1857. The outer circumstances are well known: his relationship with Mathilde Wesendonck had reached its crisis; moreover, the prospect of having the *Ring* performed in the way he visualised it seemed still remote. So he broke off the composition in the second act of *Siegfried* to produce a work which could be easily performed at one of the regular opera houses. The result was *Tristan und Isolde*.

In his Epilogue to the publication of the *Ring,* Wagner draws a parallel between Tristan and Siegfried. He speaks of the "great connection of all genuine myths" and compares the relationship of Tristan to Isolde with that of Siegfried to Brünnhilde. "The similarity consists in the fact that both Tristan and Siegfried woo the woman destined for them by primordial law on behalf of another man, forced by a delusion that makes this act an unfree one, and that they meet their end owing to the resulting conflict." (VI, 268). The comparison is not very convincing. It is one of Wagner's attempts to proffer a theoretical explanation for his creative work. In fact, with *Tristan und Isolde* he turned his back on Germanic myth for good and reverted to medieval legend, that is, to the sphere of *Tannhäuser* and *Lohengrin,* though on an infinitely higher plane. From now on there are no more gods and other super- or subhuman creatures, only human beings with their conflicts, passions, and sufferings.

Wagner's source for *Tristan und Isolde* was Gottfried von Strassburg's 13th century epic poem *Tristan,* which in turn was based on earlier French and Celtic versions of the story. But his treatment was very different from that applied in the

Ring tetralogy. Instead of presenting the entire epic in visible action, he reduced it to its bare essence, the love and death of the two protagonists. We are told nothing of Tristan's origin and youth, his numerous exploits and combats, nor of his involvement with another Isolde "of the white hands"—in short, of the whole external action related in the epic. The entire story is condensed into three crucial episodes: the drinking of the love-potion, the discovery of the lovers ending in Tristan's fatal wound, and the lovers' death.

Structurally, the drama is built on strictly classical lines reminiscent of French tragedy. There are five characters, symmetrically arranged: the triangle Tristan-Isolde-Marke, and the two lovers' confidants, Kurwenal and Brangäne. All external action is eliminated, or rather, it is internalised in the dialogue, reduced to its bare essentials. Here Wagner's art of transforming epic into drama reaches its peak.

The complex history preceding the drama, told in vivid detail in the epic poem, is first touched upon in Kurwenal's mocking song in Act I, which, rendered in prose, runs: "Sir Morold went across the sea to collect tribute from Cornwall. He now lies buried on an island floating in the sea, but his head is in Ireland, paid as a tribute by England," and concludes with the refrain, repeated by the crew: "Hail to our hero, Tristan! How well he can pay tribute!" This alludes to a long sequence of events, described in the epic: the kingdoms of Cornwall and England, subjected by Ireland, had to pay annual tribute. When Duke Morold, brother of the Irish queen, came to collect the tribute, he was challenged by King Marke's nephew, Tristan. In their combat, fought on a small island in the Irish Sea, Tristan slew Morold but was himself gravely wounded. Morold's body was buried on the island while his head was sent in defiance to Ireland. Further events from the epic are indicated in the dialogue between Isolde and Brangäne, particularly in Isolde's account *von einem Kahn* . . . "of a boat, small and poor, floating by Ireland's shore, wherein a sick man lay, wretched and dying . . ." Tristan, suffering from the wound he had received in his fight with Morold, asked to be sent to hostile Ireland, whose queen was famous for her medical skill. Arriving in a small skiff, in the guise of a minstrel and under the assumed name of Tantris, he was taken to the court and cured by the queen. In Wagner's drama, it is the young Isolde herself who, moved by pity, has cured him. Wagner also telescopes Tristan's two visits to Ireland: in Gottfried's poem, it is only on his second journey, undertaken to woo Isolde for King Marke, that she recognises him as the slayer of Morold by a splinter of his sword found in Morold's head, and by unravelling his assumed name, Tantris. Moreover, while in the original Morold is merely the queen's brother, that is, Isolde's uncle, Wagner makes him her betrothed. So her vow to avenge Morold's death is more deeply motivated. Similarly, her failure to kill Tristan when he was in her power assumes greater significance. In Gottfried's epic, she finds him in the bath and, as she is about to strike him, is held back by her mother and Brangäne. In Wagner's version, this episode is given a different turn, as she describes it to Brangäne: "From his bed he looked at me—not at the sword nor at my hand—he looked into my eyes. I took pity on his misery, and dropped the sword." What she believes to be pity was of course, unknown to herself, the first stirring of her love. By thus deepening the emotional relationship between the two, Wagner heightens the tragic involvement and provides a motive for Isolde giving Tristan a death potion to avenge Morold's death. But she, too, is resolved to die—ostensibly because she feels humiliated at being made to marry a vassal king, but in truth because she is deeply hurt that Tristan has dared to woo her on behalf of another man. "Death to both of us!" she cries in a frenzy. Against her will, she discloses her true feelings: when Brangäne praises Marke's nobility and kindness, Isolde mutters half to herself:

> Ungeminnt
> den hehrsten Mann
> stets mir nah' zu sehen, –
> wie könnt' ich die Qual bestehen!

> (To see the noblest man
> unloved

for ever near me –
how could I bear this torment!)

Brangäne believes she is speaking of King Marke, whereas of course she has Tristan in mind.

As for the crucial potion itself, Wagner has significantly changed its original function. In the epic poem, the drinking of the love philtre is a mere accident: the queen has secretly entrusted it to Brangäne to give to Marke and Isolde on their wedding-night. On board ship, while Brangäne is absent, some young ladies-in-waiting, ignorant of its powers, offer it to Tristan and Isolde. When Brangäne returns she realises what has happened and, deeply shocked, flings the empty flask into the sea. There is no question of a death potion (though Tristan, on hearing what they have drunk, exclaims light-heartedly: "Whether it be life or death, it has poisoned me most sweetly!")

It is well known how Wagner has enriched the climactic moment: Brangäne, ordered by Isolde to prepare the death potion, surreptitiously substitutes the love potion. When Tristan has drunk part of it, Isolde snatches the cup from him and with the cry, "Half of it mine!" empties it. Whereupon the two, believing they are about to die, become conscious of their love and confess it to one another. The subtle psychology underlying this sudden transformation has often been commented on: even if there were no power in the potion, the belief that they had drunk their death would force their love into the open. From the very start, love and death, the two themes of the drama, are inextricably intertwined.

In the medieval poem, the two already consummate their love on the journey. It is for this reason that they conceive the plan of substituting Brangäne for Isolde on the wedding-night. In Wagner's drama there is no need for this ruse: at the very moment the couple drink the potion the coast of Cornwall is sighted, and as the lovers stand transfixed the ship's crew cheer their happy landfall—a masterstroke of dramatic irony, on which the curtain falls.

The second act, opening on Isolde's rapt expectation of her love, is given over to the great love duet, which is interrupted

Woodcuts from *Volksbuch*, Augsburg, 1484.

Tristan arrives in Ireland.

King Marke discovers Tristan and Isolde.

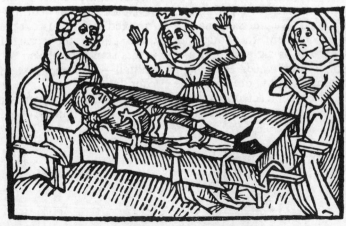

Isolde laments the death of Tristan.

by Marke's return from the hunt. It ends with the fatal wound Tristan receives at the hands of Melot. This, too, is a radical foreshortening of a long series of events related in the epic poem—the unclouded enjoyment of their love by the happy pair, the growing suspicion of a courtier, Marjodoc, the endless vacillations of the king, Tristan's banishment from the court, and so on. All this Wagner compresses into a single night. He also merges two characters, Marjodoc and the court-dwarf Melot, into one, making Melot Tristan's closest friend who turns traitor. Tristan's challenge is a clear attempt at suicide: he deliberately drops his sword before Melot strikes.

The third act belongs almost entirely to the dying Tristan waiting for Isolde's ship to arrive, alternating between utter despair and feverish ecstasy. (In the medieval romance, Tristan dies from a poisoned wound received in a fight unrelated to his love for Isolde—another instance of Wagner's ingenious tightening of the story). Now Kurwenal, who has hardly appeared before, comes into his own as the loyal servant who all but shares his master's agonies and in the end dies for him—surely one of Wagner's most moving creations. Isolde's *Liebestod*, which closes the work, is clearly prefigured in the original legend; but in the drama it assumes a new, metaphysical dimension.

The three acts of the drama are symmetrically divided between the two protagonists: the first is dominated by Isolde, the second belongs to both, while the third is almost exclusively Tristan's. King Marke, on the other hand, has only one scene to himself (apart from the end, when he arrives too late to bring Tristan his forgiveness). This scene, after the discovery of the lovers, consists virtually of one long monologue in which the king addresses only Tristan, never Isolde. It is Tristan's deceit that has struck him to the heart. The tone of his speech is sorrowful rather than angry. Where have loyalty and honour fled since Tristan, the very paragon of knightly virtue, has betrayed him? He recalls that it was Tristan who urged him to marry Isolde and who insisted on wooing her on his behalf. What, he asks, is "the impenetrably deep mysterious ground" for this betrayal? Tristan, who has been silent all along, is unable to answer: "Oh king, that—I cannot tell you; and what you ask you can never learn." Marke's incomprehension at Tristan's betrayal re-echoes Brünnhilde's when she believes herself deceived by Siegfried. And like Brünnhilde, he learns too late that what he thought to be a wilful breach of faith was in fact the result of a potion—the love potion in Tristan's case, the drink of oblivion in Siegfried's. Both are, in a deeper sense, innocent victims of outer circumstances. When Marke, enlightened by Brangäne about the love philtre, arrives at the close of the drama, ready to forgive the lovers and unite them in marriage, he finds Tristan dead and Isolde stretched unconscious over his body. The tragedy has run its course.

In the letter informing Liszt of his project of *Tristan und Isolde,* Wagner calls it "a musical conception". Two years later, in 1856, he writes to Marie Wittgenstein that while composing *Siegfried* he has inadvertently got into *Tristan,* as yet writing music without words. And early the following year, he sent Mathilde Wesendonck a piece of music without any words. So the creative process was reversed for once. In fact, in no other work of Wagner is the music so predominant or, to put it another way, does the text form merely the basis for the music. This procedure seems to contradict Wagner's own theories as he had established them in his earlier writings. He was well aware of it himself: in his essay *Zukunftmusik (Music of the Future),* written in 1860, after the completion of the work, he declares that, while creating *Tristan,* "I moved at last with full freedom and with total disregard of any theoretical considerations, in such a way that I myself realised during the work how far I had outgrown my system." (VII, 119).

This new approach affects the form, indeed the very language of the text. Not only is it almost devoid of external action, the situations are virtually static, with the few climactic moments—the drinking of the potion, Tristan's fight with Melot, the death of the lovers—compressed at the end of each act. The language, too, differs greatly from that of the *Ring.* There is only occasional alliteration; the dialogue is in short verses, often rhymed, and clearly adapted to its musical purpose. In fact, one can hardly speak of dialogue: the words of the lovers, from the moment they are aware of their feelings, are virtually interchangeable and are in fact frequently interchanged. Tristan and Isolde *(das süsse Wörtlein 'und')* have literally become one, each having lost his or her individuality. The death of one necessitates the death of the other: this is the true meaning of Isolde's *Liebestod*.

The drama is as much a glorification of death as of love—indeed, more so. In this sense, the love philtre is just as much a death-potion, as the lovers are both aware. But death for them is the redeemer, the longed-for deliverer from the delusions and sufferings of life. The whole great love duet revolves around the antithesis of life and death, symbolised in day and night, light and darkness. The torch Isolde extinguishes as a sign to her lover is also a symbol of death. In his dying words, Tristan alludes to it: *Die Leuchte–ha! Die Leuchte erlischt!* (The torch—the torch goes out!). The summons to love is also a summons to death. In their long duologue, the lovers reiterate in countless variations the dialectic of day and night. The day is treacherous, hateful, full of delusion and deceit *(Wahn* and *Trug)*; only "the blissful realm of night" *(das Wonnereich der Nacht)* promises peace and oblivion. This is also the theme of the central passage of the love duet *O sink' hernieder* . . . "Oh descend, night of love, give oblivion that I live, take me into your womb, detach me from the world . . ." When they have been overtaken by the return of Marke, Tristan turns to Isolde, asking her if she will follow him "to the dark, nocturnal land from where my mother sent me out." Life is a brief awakening into the odious day, encircled by night. Similarly, in the third act, the dying Tristan curses the sun which still forces him to suffer the light of day. Finally, Isolde's *Liebestod*: here the words, as it were·disembodied, strung together merely by assonance and rhyme, suggest the submersion of consciousness into blissful oblivion, in other words, the willing transition into—Nirvana.

It is evident that the whole work is steeped in the spirit of Schopenhauer, using in fact some of his very terminology.

However, there is a crucial contradiction. Schopenhauer denigrates sexual love as the extreme expression of the "Will to Life", that is of the Will of the world working through the individual to propagate the species: Wagner was well aware of the contradition between this concept and a work dedicated throughout to the glorification of love. With his usual urge for theoretical justification, he attempted to re-interpret and assimilate Schopenhauer's life-negating philosophy to his own purposes. This attempt is clearly reflected in the entry in his diary on 1st December, 1858, while he was working on *Tristan*: "I recently read once again friend Schopenhauer's chief work, and this time he has stimulated me to expand and—in details—even rectify his system . . . It is a question of indicating the road of salvation—recognised by no philosopher, nor indeed by Schopenhauer—to complete quieting of the Will through love, not an abstract love of men but love actually springing from sexual love, that is, affection between man and woman. It is decisive for me to be able to employ (as a philosopher, not as a poet, for as such I have my own) the material of concepts Schopenhauer himself gives me." (Wagner/Wesendonk, 149). Wagner even embarked on a letter to the philosopher, using Schopenhauer's own heading "Metaphysics of Sexual Love", evidently with the intention of imparting his own views on the subject. (The letter was apparently never completed, but a fragment has been included in Wagner's Collected Works. (XII, 291).)

Schopenhauer is of course only one spiritual source of *Tristan und Isolde*. The other, reaching further back, is German Romanticism, with its affinity to night and death, its emphasis on the inner world of dream and ecstasy. There are striking parallels between the words of the love duet and Novalis' *Hymns to Night*. Thus Wagner's work stands at a crossroad between past and future: it is the supreme culmination of Romanticism, and it indicates, in musical terms, the dissolution of tonality—the beginning of modern music. But that is another story.

VII

MASTERSHIP:
DIE MEISTERSINGER VON NÜRNBERG

No one who had followed Wagner's evolution up to this point could have guessed that he would ever write anything like *Die Meistersinger von Nürnberg (The Mastersingers of Nuremberg)*, his only comic opera (not counting *Das Liebesverbot*). Yet the idea of this work was in his mind over a long period of time: it went back to the summer of 1845 when, worn-out by his work on *Tannhäuser,* he sought to recover at Marienbad. "Without knowing much about Sachs and his contemporary poets," he writes in *My Life,* "I invented on a walk a funny scene, in which the cobbler, as a popular artisan-poet, gives the Marker a lesson with the hammer on the last, in retaliation for some pedantic misdeeds of the latter." He also envisaged a streetbrawl in a narrow Nuremberg lane to end the second act—"and suddenly my whole Mastersinger comedy stood vividly before me." (XIV, 115–6). The first prose draft already contains in full detail the entire action of the opera—still without names except for Hans Sachs, David, and Magdalene. Stolzing is "a young man, son of an impoverished knight," later simply "the lover", Eva "a rich burgher's girl", Beckmesser just "the Marker". The whole plan, culminating in a song contest, was envisaged as a comic counterpart to *Tannhäuser,* like the satyr play following a Greek tragedy. For the time being, however, this project was shelved in favour of *Lohengrin,* which was more in keeping with Wagner's serious mood at the time. Sixteen years elapsed before he returned to it—after completing *Tristan*—now in his full maturity and at a very different stage of his artistic development.

In the autumn of 1861, on a short visit to Venice, he conceived the plan of working out *Die Meistersinger* as a grand comic opera. In quick succession he produced two more prose sketches. He also compiled, from a close study of historical sources, the names of the leading mastersingers, their intricate rules and customs, the names of their various tunes—in short, the whole historical background to be absorbed in the opera. The two prose drafts correspond in almost every detail to the final work—except for the names of the main characters: Walther appears as "Konrad", Eva as "Emma", her father as "Bogner", Magdalene is called "Kathrine", while the Marker is given the name of "Hanslich"—an obvious hit at the Viennese critic Hanslick, a notorious adversary of Wagner*.

At last, in the winter of 1862, he completed the whole text in Paris within thirty days. On his forty-ninth birthday, he wrote to Mathilde Wesendonck: "It has now become clear to me that this work is going to be my most perfect masterpiece." (Wagner/Wesendonk, 399) He was conscious of the irony of writing this most German of all his works in the French capital, while looking from his window at the Tuileries and the Louvre, as far as the Hôtel de Ville. The great tune of Hans Sachs's poem on the Reformation, *Wach' auf!*, came to him while he was passing through the Palais Royal on his way to the Taverne Anglaise. Thus his situation was very much like that of his first stay in Paris, twenty years earlier, when his disappointments had aroused in him an intense longing for Germany and all things German.

Although the plot of *Die Meistersinger* was largely of Wagner's own invention, it was evidently stimulated by a tale

---

* In *My Life* Wagner reports that he read the completed text to a circle of friends in Vienna, which included Hanslick: "We noticed in the course of the reading that the dangerous critic grew more and more moody and pale, and it struck us that after I had finished he couldn't be induced to stay any longer but soon took his leave in an unmistakably irritable tone of voice. My friends agreed that Hanslick regarded the whole poem as a squib directed at him, and had taken our invitation to the reading as an insult." (XV, 341–2)

of E.T.A. Hoffmann, his favourite writer, who had repeatedly served him as a source, *Meister Martin, der Küfner, und seine Gesellen (Master Martin, the Cooper, and his Journeymen)*. The story is about a Nuremberg craftsman, a cooper, who has vowed to give his pretty daughter to the man who could produce a perfect vat as his masterpiece. Three young journeymen compete for the prize, though one of them is in fact a painter, the next a silversmith, the third a knight in disguise. Eventually the one with whom the girl is in love produces the vat and wins her hand. More important than this plot is the vivid evocation of the background, 16th century Nuremberg with its civic pride, its respect for art and craftsmanship. Even the Mastersingers play a part, as two of the journeymen attend their meetings in St. Catherine's Church and hope to join them one day as fully fledged Masters. There can be little doubt that Wagner drew on this story, possibly even in the central action of Pogner, the goldsmith, promising his daughter as a prize in the song contest.

In every respect *Die Meistersinger von Nürnberg* is in complete contrast to *Tristan und Isolde*. While the latter is wholly introverted, centring on two individuals utterly absorbed in themselves and consciously detached from the world around them, the former presents this world in a rich and colourful panorama; while *Tristan* celebrates death and the death-wish, *Die Meistersinger* is from beginning to end life-affirming. Outwardly, their three act structure—day-night-day—is similar, but in *Tristan* the day is odious, a source of unending suffering, while in *Die Meistersinger* it is radiant with happiness and festive joy. Nevertheless, there are links between the two works, of which more shall be said presently.

Die Meistersinger is the only work of Wagner (except *Rienzi*) precisely defined in time and place—16th century Nuremberg. It is his only realistic work, without a hint of myth or of any supernatural powers. Nevertheless it is quite in keeping with his fundamental belief in the *Volk* as the true creator of art: it is the people who have taken Hans Sachs to their hearts, hailing him with his own poem, and it is the

Nuremberg at the time of Hans Sachs, woodcut, 1527.

1 5 4 5 : HANS . SACHS N . ALER . 5 I . IAR

Hans Sachs, woodcut by Michael Ostendorfer, 1545.

people who acclaim Walther as victor in the song contest. But this *Volk* is seen here quite realistically, as the citizens of Nuremberg at a given historical moment—the German Reformation.*

However, there is a palpable link with the period in which Wagner has set most of his works, the German Middle-Ages, in the figure of Walther von Stolzing. Wagner describes him as "a young son of a knight who, inspired by his reading of heroic romances and the old Minnesingers, has left his impoverished and dilapidated ancestral castle to learn the art of the Mastersingers in Nuremberg." (IV, 285). When asked who his teacher was, he names Walther von der Vogelweide. "A good master!" says Sachs, to which Beckmesser interjects: "But long since dead!" (in fact, about 300 years!) There is a touch of the hero in Stolzing himself: he is for ever ready to draw his sword—even at the Nightwatchman, when he sees his elopement frustrated. Thus Stolzing is something of an anachronism in 16th century Nuremberg.

Paradoxically, the Mastersingers themselves, flourishing in the German cities from the 15th century onwards, aspired to revive the medieval Minnesong. But since they were composed throughout of plain craftsmen's guilds, their art soon degenerated to a set of rules and regulations with little genuine artistic inspiration. The only exception was Hans Sachs, the Nuremberg shoemaker (1494-1576), whose numerous poems and plays—above all his Shrovetide plays taken from everyday life—show rich imagination and a rough-and-ready humour. He has been made the subject of several poetic works, such as a play by the 19th century Austrian playwright Deinhardstein, for which Goethe wrote

* Of one project which occupied Wagner some years later, in 1868, little more is known than the title: *Luthers Hochzeit (Luther's Wedding)*. Its theme was evidently the challenging act of Luther, the Augustinian monk, in breaking his vow of celibacy and marrying a nun, Katharine. Although nothing remains of this plan, the very fact that Wagner contemplated it at all is intriguing. It shows that he felt so deeply involved in the age of the German Reformation that he envisaged another work, this time centring on the great reformer himself, "the Wittenberg Nightingale" of Hans Sachs's poem. However, nothing came of this project although Wagner is said to have returned to it later, at the time of *Parsifal*.

a prologue in 1828, and on which Lortzing based the opera *Hans Sachs* of 1840. Goethe also wrote a poem *Hans Sachs's Poetic Mission,* inspired by an old woodcut. But it is Wagner's opera which has accorded the shoemaker-poet immortal fame.

The language of *Die Meistersinger* is modelled on the language of Hans Sachs's own plays—irregular rhymed couplets, known in German as *Knittelvers,* a kind of doggerel. It must be borne in mind that while in English this verse—the verse of the Miracle plays and Moralities down to *Everyman*—has been utterly devalued, in German it has retained its full force: Germany's greatest drama, *Faust,* is for the greater part written in it, and it has been effectively employed to this day.* Wagner handles this verse with great skill, exploiting its rich potentialities from pithy dialogue to full lyrical expression.

The dramatic structure shows Wagner's theatrical mastery at its most accomplished. Since the action is not derived, like most of his other works, from an epic source, but is entirely of his own invention, the drama is free from the recapitulations of past events which so often retard the dramatic progress. The play opens with the meeting of the lovers in church, followed by the scene in which David initiates Stolzing in the rules of the Mastersingers, the assembly of the Mastersingers for their morning session, the announcement of the coming song contest, the introduction of Stolzing, and his failure in the test song: the whole conflict unfolds before our eyes, set against the background of the Mastersingers' customs. Moreover, the characters of the individual Mastersingers are at once clearly established: Pogner's noble dignity, Beckmesser's garrulity and growing animosity, Sachs's warmhearted humanity and open-mindedness towards Stolzing's unorthodox art. The culmination of Wagner's plot is undoubtedly the second act, pervaded by the magic of the summer night. The central situation must be one of the most ingenious in all comedy: the two lovers, ready to elope, are

---

* Typical examples are Hofmannsthal's *Everyman,* and, more recently, Günter Grass's *The Plebians Rehearse an Uprising* and Peter Weiss's *Marat/Sade* and *Hölderlin.*

constantly thwarted, first by the Nightwatchman on his round, then by Beckmesser singing his song to what he believes is Eva, but is in fact Magdalene who has changed clothes with her. All along Sachs, resolved to prevent the elopement, sits in front of his workshop, singing his cobbler's song and playing his game with Beckmesser, who in turn pretends to sing his song for Sachs's approval. Finally, David, recognising Magdalene at the window, rushes out to beat up Beckmesser, leading to a free fight involving the whole neighbourhood. The third act is divided into two contrasting scenes: the first, in Sachs's workshop, deepens and resolves the relationships between the main characters, while the second presents the whole panorama of the folk festival, culminating in the song contest and the acceptance of Stolzing as a Mastersinger.

The action takes place within twenty-four hours leading to the feast of St. John. Throughout the play, this feast with its associations of baptism is touched upon: as the curtain rises, the congregation sings an anthem to the "Baptist, Christ's forerunner"; Pogner in his address to the Mastersingers announces his plan of the prize-song for tomorrow's festival; the apprentices, at the beginning of Act II, sing their merry round in praise of St. John's Night; David, in Act III, recites his homely song about St. John standing by the Jordan and discovers that it is also Hans Sachs's nameday; finally, the idea of baptism is invoked by Sachs in his speech preceding the quintet as he humorously christens Stolzing's song:

> *Ein Kind ward hier geboren;*
> *jetzt sei ihm ein Nam' erkoren.*

> (*A child was born here,*
> *now let us choose a name for it*)

The central figure is of course Hans Sachs. Recalling his first conception of the work, Wagner writes: "I conceived Hans Sachs as the last manifestation of the artistically productive spirit of the people (*Volksgeist*), in contrast to the Mastersingers' philistinism, to whose comic, tabulature-poetic pedantry I gave a quite personal expression in the figure of the Marker." (IV, 284-5). Hans Sachs and Beckmesser thus represent the two sides of the Mastersingers' art—the one rooted in the *Volk*, the other alienated from it by artificial rules. However, both of them are no mere abstractions but characters of flesh and blood, with their personal conflicts and idiosyncracies. In his first speech at the Mastersingers' assembly, Sachs emphasises the importance of the *Volk* as a judge of art. Pogner has suggested that Eva should marry only the one to whom the masters have accorded the prize. To which Sachs objects that "a woman's heart and the masters' art" don't always see eye to eye: "Let the people, too, be judge—they will surely agree with the girl." In other words: the untutored sense of the *Volk* will be at one with the instinct of woman. When the masters protest that their rules would go for nothing, he proposes that once a year these rules should be tested by those who don't know anything about them—only then will their art remain truly popular. He concludes with the couplet:

Dass Volk und Kunst gleich blüh' und wachs',
Bestellt ihr so, mein' ich, Hans Sachs.

(Thus you'll make sure that Volk *and Art will*
        flourish together,
So think I, Hans Sachs.)

The reconciliation of rules with free expression is Sachs's main artistic concern—as it was Wagner's when he came to write *Die Meistersinger*. When Walther sings his test song *Fanget an! So rief der Lenz . . .* (Begin! Thus called the spring . . .) which is one single lyrical outpouring disdaining all rules, Sachs is the only one who listens attentively, admiring the singer's courage and poetic inspiration; but his words are drowned by the indignant uproar of the others. In his first great monologue (the *Fliedermonolog*) Sachs reflects on Walther's song. He feels instinctively that it was "right", though it contradicted all rules:

Kein' Regel wollte da passen,
und war doch kein Fehler drin.

(No rule would fit it,
yet there was no mistake in it.)

He likens it to birdsong; it was *Lenzes Gebot, die süsse Not,* the sweet bidding of spring, that inspired the singer!

The synthesis of free expression and traditional rules is the main theme of Sachs's instructions to Stolzing on how to shape his prize song. Anybody, he explains, can sing a song when young and on fire with love and spring. But only the masters' rules, learnt in good time, will help him preserve what love and spring have poured into his heart. He then proceeds, as Walther puts his dream into words, to lead him gently along: the second stanza must be equal to the first, as the right wife is equal to her husband, to be followed by the *Abgesang*—a third stanza which must be "similar but not equal" to the first two, as the child is to his parents.

In this way Sachs shapes and channels Stolzing's intuitive outpourings to conform to the rules of the Mastersingers. When at the end of the opera Stolzing defiantly rejects the title of Mastersinger, Sachs in his final address stresses the significance of their tradition: whatever their faults, they have preserved the dignity of art against all dangers and pressures, therefore: "Honour your German masters!" Thus Sachs reconciles "free expression", represented by Stolzing, with "form", as imposed by the Mastersingers— just as Wagner himself reconciles his revolutionary inno- vations in musical language with classical form in the work as a whole.

Artistic issues concern of course only one side of Hans Sachs's rich personality. The other is his personal involve- ment in the love between Walther and Eva. It is this that gives him his true human stature. We learn that he is a widower who has lost his wife and children, and that there is an unspoken understanding that he will marry Eva one day. When Eva approaches him, in Act II, and, hearing that Walther has failed in his test song, bursts out in bitter recrimination against the Mastersingers, Sachs realises that she is in love with the knight and quietly resolves to help the young couple. But when he discovers their plan to elope, he does all in his power to prevent it. His true feelings are revealed in Act III, when Eva comes to his workshop under the pretext that her shoes are hurting, but in fact to find out what has happened to Walther. As the knight enters dressed for the festival and the lovers lose themselves in one another's sight, Sachs pretends not to see him and breaks out in an angry diatribe against his job as a cobbler—in reality only to hide his pain. Eva, deeply touched, confesses that had it not been for Walther, she would certainly have married him; Sachs, however, recalls the sad story of Tristan and Isolde, and concludes:

> *Hans Sachs war klug, und wollte*
> *nichts von Herrn Markes Glück.*

> *(Hans Sachs was wise and wanted*
> *none of Sir Marke's luck.)*

This explicit reference to his preceding work sums up Wagner's own development to maturity and resignation.

Thus Sachs shows his wisdom in the influence he exerts over Walther in love as in art. He guides the young couple towards marriage, restraining their romantic impulse to elope, just as he leads Walther to bring his unfettered lyrical outpourings within the confines of art. The ultimate union of the young lovers parallels the artistic synthesis Walther has discovered with the help of Sachs.

The innermost core of Hans Sachs's personality is revealed in his great monologue in Act III, known as the *Wahnmonolog*. In its first word, *Wahn,* repeated three times, Wagner uses his favourite term, derived from Schopenhauer, for folly, madness, illusion. Sachs sees it everywhere. However much he has searched in ancient chronicles to discover why men torment one another and in doing so hurt only themselves, he can find only one reason—*Wahn*. What, he muses, made the peaceful citizens of Nuremberg suddenly fall upon each other in blind fury on St. John's Night? "A glow-worm couldn't find his mate—he has caused the mischief!" But there is also another, positive side to *Wahn*: if subtly guided, it can produce noble works. And Sachs resolves to use *Wahn* for this very purpose.*

If Sachs is at one with the *Volk,* who greet him with his own poem on the Reformation, *Wach' auf! es nahet gen dem Tag* . . . (Awake! The day is dawning . . .), Beckmesser represents mannered art, alienated from the people. He stands at the opposite end of the Mastersingers' range, well versed in their rules, a keen observer of their traditions, but devoid of any genuine feeling or poetic gift. In fact, it seems hardly plausible that he has ever attained the position he holds in their ranks. He moves on an altogether different level from all the other characters: he is pure caricature, narrow-minded and spiteful from the very first word he utters. His two songs—his own serenade which he sings in Act II under Eva's window and his grotesque distortion of Stolzing's prize song—are plain farce. In creating this figure, Wagner evidently aired his bitterness at all the critics who stood in his way (though he wisely erased the reference to a specific critic, Hanslick). Yet even Beckmesser has his redeeming features: when he has obtained what he believes to be Sachs's song, he embraces the cobbler happily, promising to buy his poetic works and even to yield him his place as Marker. After he has left in a whirl of joy, Sachs muses: "I have found no man quite malicious—he can't keep it up for long . . . A weak hour comes for everyone: then he'll be dumb, and you can talk to him . . ." And he slily plans to use Beckmesser for his scheme of bringing Walther and Eva together.

Eva embodies the ideal of a German maiden (as the Germans like to imagine her), with a touch of Goethe's Gretchen. Her first meeting with Walther in St. Catherine's recalls Gretchen's encounter with Faust on her way from church. She has obviously fallen in love at first sight, for she saw him only "yesterday" for the first time. But, as she confesses to Magdalene, she had been prepared through Dürer's picture of the young David challenging Goliath—a parallel to Senta's fascination by a portrait of the Dutchman.

* It is worth remembering that Wagner named his house in Bayreuth, where he finally found a home after his restless wanderings, *Wahnfried*— peace, or rest, from illusion.

Die Meistersinger: Eva and Hans Sachs, engraving after Josef
Flüggen, 1878.

Impetuously, she exclaims in her first exchanges with the knight that she will marry "you or no one!" With the same impulsiveness she is ready to elope with him that very night. But Eva's character is not quite as naïve as it appears at first sight. In Act II, she uses all her feminine wiles to get Sachs to tell her about the outcome of Walther's test song. Why shouldn't Sachs, a widower, win her in the song contest? Hadn't he carried her in his arms when she was a child? "So I thought you might take me into your house as a wife and a child." How would he like it if Beckmesser were to snatch her away from under his nose? In fact, of course, all her thoughts are fixed only on Walther. Eva, too, has her great moment: in Act III, when Sachs breaks out in his complaint against his lot as a cobbler, she sees through his pretence and addresses him in what is perhaps the most poignant passage of the whole work:

> *O Sachs! Mein Freund!* . . .
> *Was ohne deine Liebe,*
> *was wär' ich ohne dich,*
> *ob je auch Kind ich bliebe,*
> *erwecktest du nicht mich?*
>> *Durch dich gewann ich,*
>> *was man preist . . .*
>> *durch dich nur dacht'*
> *ich edel, frei und kühn;*
>> *. . . hatte ich die Wahl,*
>> *nur dich erwählt' ich mir:*
>> *du warest mein Gemahl,*
>> *den Preis nur reicht ich dir!*
>> *doch nun hat's mich gewählt*
>> *zu nie gekannter Qual:*
>> *und werd' ich heut' vermählt,*
>> *so war's ohn' alle Wahl!*

(O Sachs! My friend! . . .
What would I be without you, without your love?
Even as a child, did you not awaken me?
Through you I have gained all that is worthwhile,

> *Only through you have I thought what is noble,*
> *free, and bold! . . .*
> *. . . Had I the choice, I would choose only you!*
> *You would be my husband, I'ld give the*
> *prize only to you.*
> *But now it has chosen me for a torment never*
> *known before:*
> *And when I will be married today, it will be without*
> *any choice of my own!)*

This outbreak reveals that Eva has grown to maturity under Sachs's influence. After this climactic moment, her part has really come to an end: she only leads the great quintet—intoning the melody of Walther's prize song—and, finally, crowns him as the victor.

Of all Wagner's main characters, Walther von Stolzing comes nearest to the stereotype operatic hero. He is an outsider in Nuremberg's closely knit society, hailing from a different social stratum, the declining feudal nobility, and reared in the traditions of a past age, medieval chivalry. He is impulsive in his reactions, both in love and in anger, to anybody who crosses his way. But he, too, matures under the guidance of Hans Sachs, and in the end conforms to the order he is invited to join. Seen in a wider context, he embodies as it were an earlier stage in Wagner's own development: the romantic artist, who, defying all rigid conventions, relies only on his intuition. (His first test song is virtually an improvisation, composed on the spur of the moment.) His development to an accepted Mastersinger reflects Wagner's own.

The triangle Stolzing-Eva-Sachs repeats to a certain extent that of Siegmund-Sieglinde-Hunding and of Tristan-Isolde-Marke. But now the point of gravity has shifted: it is no longer the solitary outsider, the romantic lover, who stands at the centre, but the mature man, firmly settled in a well-ordered society. Marke has turned into Sachs, who wisely renounces his claims to a belated happiness. But Wagner is both Sachs and Stolzing; it is Stolzing who carries the message of a new art, challenging the established rules, while

Sachs channels this art into new forms, reconciling revolution and tradition, the artist and society. This is precisely the essence of *Die Meistersinger*: Wagner the revolutionary has developed into the established Master.

This development applies not only to art but also to the political sphere. *Die Meistersinger* is consciously conceived as a national work, and it has been acclaimed as such ever since. In fact, it is generally recognised as *the* national German opera. The time of its genesis had a distinct influence on the work. The year Wagner wrote the text, 1862, Bismarck was appointed Minister President of Prussia. By the time of its first performance, 1868, Prussia had won its victory over Austria and was preparing for war against France. These events and the general spirit of national consciousness they produced have clearly left their imprint on the opera. This spirit pervades *Die Meistersinger* from the very first bar. But only at the end does it become explicit in Sachs's address to the people of Nuremberg. He warns them emphatically against the dangers threatening from "false French majesty" —a veiled allusion, in its topical context, to Napoleon III, against whom the Franco-Prussian war was fought only two years later. Nevertheless, it would be wrong to see in this passage, as is often done, a mere nationalistic outburst on the part of Wagner. On a deeper level it is quite in keeping with the period of the play, the 16th century German Reformation. What Sachs prophetically foresees is the coming age of Absolutism, dominated by French influence both in politics and the arts:

> *Habt acht! Uns drohen üble Streich':-*
> *zerfällt erst deutsches Volk und Reich,*
> *in falscher wälscher Majestät*
> *kein Fürst bald mehr sein Volk versteht;*
> *und wälschen Dunst mit wälschen Tand*
> *sie pflanzen uns ins deutsche Land.*
> *Was deutsch und echt wüsst' keiner mehr,*
> *lebt's nicht in deutscher Meister Ehr'.*

(Beware! Evil blows threaten us:
Once the German people and empire disintegrate,
Soon no prince in false French* majesty
will understand his people:
and they will spread French haze and French glitter
over our German land.
No one will know any more what is German and
genuine,
if it does not live on in the worth of German masters.)

No doubt Wagner, in this final passage, voices his long-standing animosity against all things French, born of his painful experiences in Paris. However, these words should not be taken on a purely political level: they refer above all to art, as Sachs emphasises in his last lines, repeated by the whole chorus:

Zerging in Dunst
das heil'ge röm'sche Reich,
uns bliebe gleich
die heil'ge deutsche Kunst.

(Though the Holy Roman Empire
dissolve in mist,
There still remains for us
holy German Art.)

The whole of *Die Meistersinger* turns on questions of art. Wagner succeeds in presenting the essence of his theories, laid down in his theoretical writings and realised in his works, in terms of a comedy with clearly defined characters. The struggle of Walther von Stolzing against the rigid precepts of the Mastersingers reflects Wagner's own struggle against the obsolete conventions of opera. Paradoxically, he called the work an "opera", in defiance of all his previous diatribes against that art-form. However, he succeeded in integrating all its elements—arias, duets, ensembles—into the very texture of the work. Of all his operatic texts, *Die Meistersinger*

---

* Wagner says "wälsch", which generally means "foreign" but is especially applied to the Latin countries, particularly France.

von Nürnberg is perhaps the one most capable of standing on its own as a straight play—were it not for the fact that its very subject is music and the art of song.

IX

SATIRICAL INTERLUDE

The ten years between the completion of the *Meistersinger* score in 1867 and the beginning of work on *Parsifal* in 1877 saw great changes both in the outer world and in Wagner's personal life. In 1871, Germany, after the victorious Franco-Prussian War, was unified in the Empire of Bismarck. And Wagner, after completing the composition of *Siegfried* and *Götterdämmerung*, built his Bayreuth Festival Theatre and saw the first performance of the whole *Ring* cycle in 1876, with the keen participation of the entire musical world. His dreams had come true beyond expectation. The revolutionary outcast had become the established master, a symbol of the new imperial Germany.

During that period, although the idea of his last work, *Parsifal*, was intermittently in his mind, he produced only one dramatic work, an *oeuvre d'occasion*—the satirical play *Eine Kapitulation (A Capitulation)*. This slight piece, usually ignored (with some justification) in any study of Wagner's works, cannot be overlooked in an appraisal of the dramatist, all the more as Wagner himself considered it worthy of inclusion in his Collected Works. It was prompted, as "a cheerful interruption between serious works", by the patriotic mood roused by the Franco-Prussian War. Written in November 1870, when the siege of Paris had just begun, *Eine Kapitulation* envisaged the imminent surrender of that city. In this ruthless satire, Wagner gave vent to his old animosity against the French capital, resulting from his bitter disappointments during his early years and more recently from the dismal failure of the Paris production of *Tannhäuser* in 1861. His resentment found expression time and again in his published and private writings. In *A Communication to My Friends* of 1851, after his second vain attempt to gain a foothold in Paris as an exile from Germany, he wrote: "Like a black picture from a horrible long discarded past, there once more passed before me that Paris to which I had first turned on the advice of a well-meaning friend . . . , and which I now, at the first recognition of its loathsome form, rejected like a nocturnal spectre." (IV, 334). And about the same time, in a letter to his friend Uhlig he wrote tersely: "I don't believe in any revolution except one that begins with the burning of Paris." *(Sämtliche Briefe* III, 460). This wish was almost literally fulfilled in 1871. With his supreme egocentricity which related everything to himself and his work, he probably regarded the war and the fall of Paris as a just retribution for the slights he had suffered.

Wagner called *Eine Kapitulation* "a comedy in the antique manner", evidently taking Aristophanes as his model. The scene, representing the square before the Hôtel de Ville in Paris, has the shape of an ancient orchestra, the thymele being formed by an altar of the Republic with a Jacobin cap and fasces on it. The chorus is made up by the National Guard and later the rats from the Paris sewers. The two principal figures are Victor Hugo, the champion of the newly founded Republic, just returned from exile, and Jacques Offenbach, the representative of French opera and ballet, both of them appearing from the sewers underneath the city. Besides them, there are Jules Fabre, Gambetta, etc., leaders of the Republican government, who assemble on the balcony of the half-destroyed Hôtel de Ville. The point of the action is that Offenbach, "the Orpheus of the Underworld, the Piedpiper of Hamelin" will save Paris by producing his operas: "Whoever has him within his walls is for ever invincible and has the whole world for his friend!" Wagner pours his scorn on Offenbach, whom he always regarded as his extreme antipode, a symbol of French frivolity and the prostitution of operatic art. While the chorus hails him as the saviour of France, Offenbach directs the ballet, consisting of rats who have changed into "ladies of the ballet in the slightest of operatic costumes". Eventually Hugo, dressed as a genius with a golden lyre, proclaims the victory of the French over the Germans, turning the historical facts upside down. In the end he invites the Germans to enter Paris as *amis*, in order to enjoy French restaurants, theatres, opera, and so on. In a song, he declares that only by transforming them into French opera have the "pompous" German classics, *Faust, Mignon, Don Carlos, Wilhelm Tell,* become digestible. The final stage direction says that, along with the various European ambassadors, the directors of the large German court theatres join in the general gallop, directed by Offenbach.

So in the end this rather tasteless political satire turns on questions of art. The capitulation of the title is ambiguous: it refers not so much to the capitulation of Paris (which at the time of writing had not yet happened) as to the surrender of the Germans to the lure of French opera. Seen in this light, this somewhat embarrassing piece is merely the extreme expression of Wagner's lifelong struggle against the conventions of grand opera, represented by Meyerbeer, Gounod, Thomas, and others.

Eine Kapitulation has probably never been staged. As Wagner writes in the Foreword, he handed the text to a young musician of his acquaintance to write the required music to it. However, when a Berlin suburban theatre, to which the piece was anonymously offered, rejected it, the musician felt relieved, confessing that he would have found it impossible to write the necessary music à la Offenbach. "From which we recognised," Wagner concludes, "that everything requires genius and natural vocation, both of which we acknowledged in this instance wholeheartedly in Monsieur Offenbach." (IX, 4) So Wagner paid a backhanded compliment to his French opponent after all.

X

THE MYTH OF REDEMPTION:
PARSIFAL

With *Parsifal*, his last work, Wagner returned to the world of Arthurian legend, on which Tristan was based. The idea of this work had accompanied him for a long time—ever since he had made Wolfram von Eschenbach, the author of the medieval romance *Parzival*, one of the main characters of *Tannhäuser*. There he presented Wolfram not as a great epic poet but only as a Minnesinger, glorifying pure love in contrast to Tannhäuser's praise of sensuality. But shortly after, in that seminal Marienbad summer of 1845, he read Wolfram's *Parzival*; "With the book under my arm I buried myself in the nearby wood paths, in order to converse, stretched by a brook, with Titurel and Parzival in the strange yet so intimately homely poem of Wolfram." (XIV, 115). In *Lohengrin,* he drew on the last chapter of that epic for the story of Loherangrin, Parzival's son. But here the Grail itself remains on the periphery of the action, appearing only in Lohengrin's narration. The theme was taken up again in the early plan of *Tristan*, according to which Parzival, in search of the Grail, was to appear at Tristan's sickbed—a plan which was soon dropped, though *Tristan* and *Parsifal* remained linked in more ways than one.

It was only in 1857, in Zürich, that the subject returned in a flash to Wagner's mind. As he records in *My Life*: "On Good Friday I awoke for the first time in this house in full sunshine: the little garden had turned green, the birds were singing ... Full of this, I suddenly told myself that today was Good Friday, and I remembered how meaningful this admonition had struck me already once in Wolfram's *Parzival*. Since that stay in Marienbad, where I conceived *The Mastersingers* and *Lohengrin*, I had never again occupied myself with that poem; now its ideal substance occurred to me with overwhelming force, and, starting from the idea of Good Friday, I quickly conceived a whole drama, divided into three acts, which I at once sketched in outline." (XV, 134). So it is actually the Good Friday scene of Act III which formed the nucleus of the work.

From then on, the thought of Parzival never quite left Wagner, as can be seen from several letters he wrote to Mathilde Wesendonck in 1859, in the middle of composing *Tristan*, another proof of how closely the two works were linked in his mind. Strangely enough, the longest of these letters (30 May, 1859) turns on the figure of Amfortas rather than the title role: "Closely considered, Amfortas is the centre and main subject . . . It suddenly became terribly clear to me: he is my Tristan of the third act in an unthinkable intensification. A spear wound and may be yet another in his heart, the poor man in his terrible pain knows no other longing than to die . . ." Wagner goes on to expatiate eloquently on the significance of the Holy Grail, the sight of which prevents Amfortas from dying. He dismisses Wolfram's epic as a mere string of adventures, which fails to explore the deeper significance of the myth. In this poem, the Grail is merely a miraculous stone, which Wagner traces to the Mohammedan Caaba at Mecca. Only in the Christian conception of the Grail as the sacred vessel filled with Christ's blood which Joseph of Arimathea brought from the Holy Land, does it gain its full mystical significance. At the close of his letter, Wagner turns to Parzival himself: "He is indispensable as the longed-for redeemer of Amfortas: if Amfortas is to be seen in the true light due to him, he is of such immensely tragic interest that it will be difficult to work up a second main interest, and yet this main interest should turn to Parzival, if he is not to enter eventually merely as an indifferent *deus ex machina*. So Parzival's development, his sublime purification, though predestined by his deeply compassionate nature, must be placed in the foreground.

And for this I can't choose a broad plan such as was at Wolfram's disposal: I must condense everything in three main situations of drastic substance in such a way that the deep and complex content nevertheless emerges clearly and distinctly." (Wagner/Wesendonk, 206ff). The structural difficulty of balancing the two main figures of Parsifal and Amfortas has left its traces in the final work: for long stretches Parsifal remains outside the action, a passive onlooker.

In another letter to Mathilde (December 1858) Wagner writes of the third main character, Kundry: *"Parzival* has occupied me a lot: in particular a curious creation, a wonderfully world-demonic woman (the Grail's messenger) grows more and more vividly and strikingly in my mind. If ever I accomplish this poem, I should produce something very original." (Wagner/Wesendonk 164). And two years later (August 1860): "Have I told you that the fabulous wild Grail's messenger and the seductive woman of the second act are one and the same being? Since this has dawned upon me, almost all of this subject has become clear to me." (Wagner/Wesendonk, 325–6).

For the time being, *Die Meistersinger* intervened. But even before completing the music to that work in 1865, Wagner wrote a detailed prose draft of *Parzival* (as he still spelt it in accordance with the original). This draft is not divided into acts but is a continuous narrative, and, in addition, an interpretation of the characters and the thought-content of the story. However, another twelve years were to elapse before Wagner produced the full text of *Parsifal* (as he finally came to spell it) in 1877—a year after the first Bayreuth performance of the *Ring*. *Parsifal* is consciously conceived as a last work, comparable to Shakespeare's *The Tempest*, Goethe's *Faust II,* and Ibsen's *When We Dead Awaken.* And like most last works, it reiterates on a higher plane many motives from earlier works. Far from being a reversal of Wagner's evolution—as Nietzsche claimed—it is its culmination. Its basic theme, the conflict between sensuality and spirituality, sin and salvation, is also the theme of *Tannhäuser;* the myth of the Grail is anticipated in *Lohengrin;* Parsifal, the "pure fool", has much in common with the young Siegfried; Kundry, who tries to ensnare him with her charms, is another Venus—but she is also Elisabeth; the magician Klingsor, who has forsworn love and is out to destroy the knights of the Grail, recalls Alberich; and Amfortas, languishing for death, is—as Wagner himself puts it—an "intensified" Tristan, while Gurnemanz, wisely leading Parsifal to his destination, has a touch of Hans Sachs. So most of the motives and configurations of Wagner's entire work reappear in *Parsifal,* though transmuted and re-interpreted in a new context.

As he does in *Tristan,* Wagner reduces the host of characters of the epic poem to a few main figures, compressing the countless episodes of the story to "three main situations of drastic substance". Moreover, he makes Munsalvaesche, which in medieval legend has no specific location, Monsalvat in "the northern mountains of Gothic Spain", that is, on the border between the Christian and Arab worlds.* The dramatic structure is strictly symmetrical: Acts I and III correspond, each ending with the ritual of the Grail, while Act II—Klingsor's magic garden—forms a contrast. Between Acts I and III, the wanderings of Parsifal—the main content of the epic—are thought to take place. This compression requires once again lengthy recapitulations of past events. Here it is Gurnemanz who in Act I relates to the four young shield-bearers the essentials of the background story: Titurel, the first king of the Grail, has in old age appointed his son Amfortas as his successor: Amfortas, however, succumbing to the snares of a beautiful woman (Kundry), has been wounded by the sacred spear, which is now in the hand of Klingsor, the magician. The latter, unable to attain to the Grail, has in revenge created the enchanted garden to ensnare the Grail knights. Gurnemanz ends his narration by quoting the mysterious words inscribed on the Grail, which promise salvation to Amfortas, and which contain the central idea of the work:

---

* The topography of Wolfram's epic is largely imaginary, ranging over the whole known world, from the Middle East to Brittany and Wales.

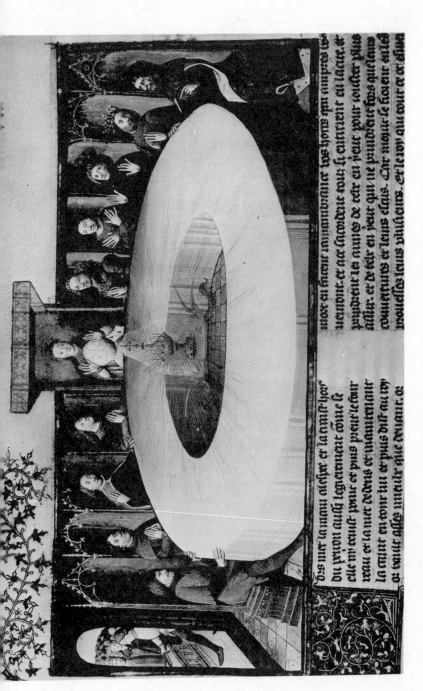

The apparition of the Holy Grail, from a 15th century manuscript of the *Conte del Graal*.

"Durch Mitleid wissend
der reine Tor,
harre sein',
den ich erkor."

(*"Knowing through compassion,*
the pure fool,
wait for him
whom I have chosen.")

This "pure fool" is Parsifal (Wagner even employs an etymologically dubious word-play by reversing his name to "fal-parsi", which he interprets as "pure fool"). When Parsifal first enters the forest adjoining Monsalvat, he has just killed one of the sacred swans in flight. As Gurnemanz shows him the dead bird, reproving him for his offence, Parsifal listens "with growing emotion" and smashes his bow—a first stirring of his "compassion", as yet mute and unconscious. To Gurnemanz's questions, who his father is, where he comes from, and what his name is, he replies: "I don't know". But when Kundry, lying hidden under a bush nearby, calls to him that his father, Gamuret, has been slain and his mother, Herzeleide, is dead, he rushes at her impulsively, intent on strangling her.

Thus Parsifal on his first appearance shows some striking affinities to Siegfried: he is born in the wilderness, his father has been killed in combat, he has grown up in the forest, fighting giants and "evil men". But there is a significant difference: unlike Sieglinde, who has preserved for Siegfried his father's broken sword, Herzeleide has brought up Parsifal "a stranger to weapons", to save him from a hero's death. His only weapons are a bow and arrows against the beasts of the forest.

Gurnemanz, suspecting that Parsifal might be the pure fool prophesied by the Grail, now leads him to the castle to attend the holy ritual: "If you are a fool and pure, let me see what knowledge is granted you."

The action now shifts to Amfortas, the other principal figure. As king of the Grail he is condemned to preside at the daily ritual of its unveiling, and so to gain, against his will, a new lease of life. In this duty he is spurred on by his aged father, Titurel, whose voice is heard "as if from a grave". (It may be argued that the introduction of that disembodied voice, rarely intelligible in performance, is dramatically superfluous. However, here Wagner faithfully follows the legend, according to which Titurel, though weary with years, is still alive. Moreover, his repeated insistence, "Unveil the Grail!" gives additional force to Amfortas' hated office). The figure of Amfortas, suffering from an incurable wound, has of course deep mythical roots reaching back to the pagan myth of the Fisher King, whose country turns into waste land simultaneously with his sickness. In Wagner's version, the Christian connotations are emphasised: the spear that has inflicted the wound is the spear, or lance, which pierced the side of Christ on the Cross. And his agonised cry for "mercy" goes out to the Redeemer, imploring Him for deliverance from his sins. Amfortas' wound has symbolic implications or, as Wagner says, he suffers "from yet another wound"—his surrender to carnal love.* This makes him indeed an "intensified" version not only of Tristan but also of Tannhäuser: both have "sinned in the flesh" and are crying out for deliverance, the one through death, the other through atonement.

The Grail having been unveiled, Amfortas is carried out, his hand on his wound, which once more has started to bleed. All the while Parsifal has silently watched the proceedings, without asking the vital question. When all have left the hall, Gurnemanz dismisses Parsifal contemptuously: "You are just a fool!" (The question is a central idea of the Grail myth. In Wolfram's poem, it is addressed to Amfortas: "What is it that ails you?" In the French *Perceval* by Chrétien de Troyes, it is a double one: "Why does the spear bleed?" and "Whom does one serve with the Grail?" On his first visit to the Grail, the hero fails to ask the question; on his second, he asks it, thus restoring Amfortas and becoming king of the Grail. Wolfram even relates the

* In Wolfram's poem, this symbolism is clearly spelt out: Amfortas is "pierced through the testicles", whereas Wagner says merely "in his side".

failure to ask this question to the forbidden question about a Grail Knight's name and origin: "Since the sweet Amfortas was so long in sore pain and went so long without the question, questioning is evermore painful to them. All those who keep the Grail want no questions asked about them." A curious and unsuspected link between *Parsifal* and the central theme of *Lohengrin*!)

The second Act centres on Klingsor and Kundry. Both figures are derived from secondary characters in the medieval epic. Clinschor (as he is called in Wolfram's poem) is a magician and owner of the Castle of Wonders who has in vain aspired to join the brotherhood of the Grail. To quell his fleshly lust, he has emasculated himself and sworn vengeance on the knights, luring them to their doom. Cundrie, on the other hand, is a sorceress of repugnant appearance, who crosses Parzival's way on several occasions. But already in the medieval legend, she is a strangely ambivalent character. She is a messenger of the Grail, often the bearer of bad tidings, but of unswerving loyalty and readiness to help. From this character, Wagner has developed one of the most enigmatic figures in all his work, and perhaps in all dramatic literature. His most ingenious stroke is to give her a dual personality. His Kundry is a beautiful seductress who tries to ensnare Parsifal, and is also gradually revealed as the one guilty of Amfortas' fall. But she is more: Wagner once compared her to the Wandering Jew. She is the *Urteufelin*, the primordial she-devil, the eternal temptress, who has appeared in many shapes through the ages: "You were Herodias, and what else? Gundryggia there, Kundry here," says Klingsor, her master. Like Ahasuerus, she lives under an eternal curse because she once laughed at the suffering Christ. To atone for her sin she humbly serves the knights of the Grail wherever she can. But at the same time she is driven to lure them to their ruin. Her reluctant servitude to Klingsor, who holds her in his power, is in fact her own compulsion to seduce whoever crosses her path. To escape this agonising conflict between two contradictory impulses, she has but one longing—sleep. Frequently she falls into a trancelike state in which her very speech consists of disjointed ejaculations: "Oh!—Oh! Deep

night! Madness!—Oh!—Rage!—Oh! Misery!—Sleep—
sleep—deep sleep!—Death!" From the depth of her soul
she, too, longs for redemption and deliverance from her curse
through death:"Eternal sleep, only salvation, how—how can
I gain you?"

In her great scene with Parsifal in Act II—the pivotal
scene of the drama—she fully reveals her ambivalent
character. Parsifal has entered Klingsor's enchanted garden
where he first dallies with the Flower maidens (not unlike
Siegfried with the Rhine maidens). Then, for the first time,
he hears himself called by his name: "Parsifal!" In the
ensuing dialogue, Kundry, now a seductive woman, tells him
of the death of his mother, Herzeleide (Heart's Sorrow) from
grief at his absence. This news stirs in Parsifal's soul the first
dim consciousness of his own folly. But Kundry quickly
passes from the theme of Parsifal's mother to a long and
passionate kiss, linking the one to the other: this "first kiss of
love", she says, is "the last greeting of a mother's blessing".
This fusion of the mother image with erotic love—clearly
foreshadowing Freudian theories—has a striking parallel in
the love scene of Siegfried and Brünnhilde: there Siegfried,
setting eyes on the sleeping Brünnhilde, instinctively invokes
his mother. And when Brünnhilde tells him that she loved
him even before he was born, he confuses her for a moment
with his mother: "So did my mother not die? Was she only
asleep?" But there the parallel ends. For while Siegfried's and
Brünnhilde's love encounter rises to its ecstatic conclusion,
Parsifal, under Kundry's kiss, suddenly remembers Amfortas. This is the decisive turning-point of his development,
marking the change from unconsciousness to consciousness,
from folly to knowlege. Tearing himself from the embrace,
he starts up "with a gesture of extreme shock":

> *Amfortas!*
> *Die Wunde! die Wunde!*
> *Sie brennt in meinem Herzen . . .*
> *Die Wunde sah ich bluten:—*
> *nun blutet sie mir selbst—*

(Amfortas!
The wound!the wound!
It burns in my heart . . .
I saw the wound bleeding:—
now it bleeds within me—)

Feeling for the first time the same "torment of love" Amfortas must have felt, he realises in a flash that it was Kundry who seduced Amfortas and caused his suffering. Now Kundry, moved by his lament, reveals to him her own predicament and the curse hanging over her. If he can feel other people's pain, why can't he also take pity on her? From time immemorial she has been waiting for him as her saviour! But she still tries to trick him: one hour of love will redeem both him and her. Parsifal pushes her away: only if she will show him the way to Amfortas can she be saved. At this she furiously summons Klingsor and his bondsmen to her aid. Klingsor appears and hurls his spear—the sacred spear he has taken from Amfortas—at Parsifal, who arrests it in mid-air and with it makes the sign of the Cross. Whereupon the castle and the enchanted garden vanish—very much like the Venusberg when Tannhäuser invokes the name of the Virgin. Parsifal's last words to Kundry are: "You know the only place where you can see me again!"

The lapse of time between this Act and the final one is undefined. We must assume that it contains the numerous adventures and combats which form the main substance of the medieval epic. When Parsifal reappears before Gurnemanz's hermitage, he is a mature man, clad in black armour, carrying the spear in his hand. It is Good Friday. This scene, which, as Wagner wrote, had been the germ of the whole work, is based on Parzival's encounter with the hermit Trevrizent in Wolfram's poem, also set on Good Friday. Gurnemanz, recognising in the stranger the youth he had once cast out from the temple of the Grail, tells him what has happened since: Amfortas, resolved to end his agony, has forbidden the Grail to be uncovered. As a result, the knights, deprived of their divine nourishment, are withering away (not unlike the gods in *Das Rheingold* lacking Freia's golden apples), and Titurel, the aged king, has died. Today the Grail is to be uncovered once more to celebrate the funeral rites. Then, recognising the sacred spear, Gurnemanz realises that Parsifal is the man destined to redeem Amfortas and become king of the Grail. All this time, Kundry, once again in the ragged garment of the Grail's messenger, has been silently present; her only words throughout the Act are: "Serve— serve!" Both she and Gurnemanz now lead Parsifal to the sacred spring; while Gurnemanz anoints his head, Kundry washes his feet and dries them with her flowing hair—a scene clearly modelled on Mary Magdalene washing the feet of Christ and foreshadowed in Wagner's own draft of *Jesus von Nazareth*. Finally Parsifal baptises Kundry and so redeems her from her curse. There follows what is known as "Good Friday Magic". As always when Wagner evokes Nature and its manifestations, his art, both poetically and musically, is at its best. How is it, asks Parsifal, that on this day of Christ's death, Nature, instead of mourning, blossoms in all its glory? Gurnemanz, in one of Wagner's finest passages, ventures an answer: Nature, moistened by the sinner's tears of repentance, looks up to man redeemed, and all her creatures enjoy this day of deliverance from guilt. In images of blossoming spring, Gurnemanz touches upon the theme of death and resurrection. Finally, as the distant bells begin to toll, the three set out for the temple of the Grail.

The final scene corresponds to the last scene of Act I: once more Amfortas is carried in, racked by pain and calling for death, while Titurel's coffin is opened. Then Parsifal enters and touches Amfortas with his spear:

> *Die Wunde schliesst*
> *der Speer nur, der sie schlug.*

> *(Only the spear that struck it*
> *can close the wound.)*

Instead of putting the question asked in the medieval epic, Parsifal relieves Amfortas by an action: the spear which was the instrument of his suffering becomes the visible symbol of compassion and redemption. When the Grail, at the

Kundry leads Parsifal to the Grail Castle, anon., 1887.

command of Parsifal, is unveiled, a white dove descends from on high and hovers over his head. (According to the legend, this dove descends from heaven once a year on Good Friday to replenish the power of the Grail). Finally Kundry, her eyes fixed on Parsifal, sinks lifeless to the ground, while Amfortas and Gurnemanz pay homage to him as their new king. With the words "Redemption for the redeemer!" intoned by distant voices, the work closes.

The drama of *Parsifal* is devoid of human conflict, moving on a purely spiritual, transcendental plane. What actions it contains are merely externalised symbols of inner states of mind. Moreover, the course of the action is predestined from the start in the formula which contains the essence of the whole work:

> Knowing through compassion,
> the pure fool . . .

All along it is clear that Parsifal is the pure fool destined to fulfil this prophesy. The drama presents no more than his progress from folly to knowledge. When, at the end of Act II, he has seized the spear—the symbol of active compassion—the drama is really at an end; the rest shows merely the carrying out of his mission. To illustrate this development, Wagner employs throughout Christian symbols—baptism, the sacred lance, the sign of the Cross, the Grail itself, being both the cup from which Christ drank at the Last Supper and the vessel containing His blood. Understandably, Wagner has been accused of misusing the most hallowed symbols of the Christian faith for theatrical purposes. He was fully aware of this risk. In a letter to King Ludwig, 28th September, 1880, he wrote: "Indeed, how can a drama in which the most sublime mysteries of the Christian faith are openly shown on the stage, be presented in theatres such as ours? I would really not blame our church authorities if they took a very justified objection to stage presentations of the holiest mysteries on the same boards as see the frivolities of yesterday and to-morrow . . . In full consciousness of this, I have called *Parsifal* a *Bühnenweihspiel* (Sacred Stage Play). I must, therefore, have a stage to dedicate to it, and this can be only my unique theatre at Bayreuth. There, and there alone, shall *Parsifal* be performed in perpetuity." (Wagner/Ludwig, III, 182). (This wish was observed, with one or two exceptions, for the legal period of thirty years, i.e. until 1913). But is *Parsifal* really a Christian work pure and simple? Is the redemption Parsifal offers identical with that of orthodox Christian doctrine? In *Religion und Kunst (Religion and Art)*—Wagner's last theoretical treatise, written in 1880, during the composition of *Parsifal*—he writes: "One could say that when religion becomes artificial, it remains for art to save the essence of religion by conceiving the mythical symbols, which religion wants us to believe to be the literal truth, according to their figurative value, in order to let us see their profound hidden truth through idealised representation. Whereas the priest is only concerned to have the religious allegories regarded as factual truths, this is of no concern to the artist, since he presents his work frankly and openly as his invention." (X, 211). Wagner thus draws a distinction between the literal use of symbols by the Church and their free application by the creative artist. In the further course of his argument, he considers the various religions, Buddhism, Judaism, Christianity, and arrives once again at Schopenhauer, whose insight he apostrophises as the "crown of all knowledge". The whole history of mankind, he argues, with its self-destroying passions and wars, is a manifestation of the Will raging against itself. What alone can redeem man, by breaking this Will, is *Liebe*—love, growing from compassion. This line of thought, which Wagner pursues in his usual rather tortuous way, points to the very essence of *Parsifal*, enshrined in the dictum "Knowing through compassion".

Compassion is indeed the key-word of the work, as it was one of Wagner's favourite terms ever since he had fallen under the spell of Schopenhauer's philosophy. In his diary, 1st October, 1858, shortly after the first conception of *Parsifal*, he elaborates to Mathilde Wesendonck his idea of compassion, calling it "the strongest trait of my moral being and probably also the source of my art". This compassion is not directed towards any individual suffering but to "the great suffering of life". More acutely than in man, it can be perceived in the speechless suffering of animals. If this suffering has any purpose it is to rouse compassion in man, who through it becomes "the world's redeemer by recognising the fallacy of all existence." "This meaning", he adds, "will one day become clear to you from the third act of *Parsifal*, on Good Friday morning." (Wagner/Wesendonk, 122–5).

Seen in this light, *Parsifal* represents the full realisation of Wagner's addiction to Schopenhauer. It is as it were the positive answer to the love-death of *Tristan und Isolde*. When Wagner, in his original plan, confronted the dying Tristan with Parsifal on the way to the Grail, he wanted no doubt to indicate two possible ways of surmounting life's suffering. In confronting Parsifal with Amfortas, he established the same contrast. What Amfortas—as well as Kundry—suffers from is not merely the sin of sexuality in the Christian sense, but life's suffering, which according to Schopenhauer can be redeemed only by compassion. As Parsifal says to Amfortas when he touches him with the spear:

> *Gesegnet sei dein Leiden,*
> *das Mitleids höchste Kraft*
> *und reinsten Wissens Macht*
> *dem zagen Toren gab.*

> *(Blessed be your suffering,*
> *which has given the supreme force of compassion*
> *and the power of purest knowledge*
> *to the timorous fool.)*

Parsifal's evolution to this purest knowledge proceeds step by step. At first, when he is shown the swan he has killed, his compassion is merely instinctive, expressed in a wordless gesture; the same applies to his first sight of Amfortas' agony at which he "convulsively touches his heart". His full awakening is brought about by Kundry's kiss: through it, he becomes *welthellsichtig* (literally, "world-clearsighted"). Finally, having acquired full knowledge, he turns it into his active deed of baptising Kundry and healing Amfortas.

"Redeem the world, if this is your office!" says Kundry. In fact, Parsifal redeems not only Amfortas and Kundry but, by reviving the power of the Grail, mankind. He thus becomes a new Saviour who—unlike Christ, who has taken the sins of the world on Himself and suffered death to redeem man—*lives on* to regenerate mankind. It could be said that Wagner has created in this work a new myth, distinctly different from the Christian myth, though using its symbols.

Parsifal begins where *Götterdämmerung* ends. While Siegfried, the free man acting on his own free will, brings about his own destruction and the end of the gods, Parsifal, through his living example, saves the world. The *hero* has been replaced by the *saint*. The theme of "Redemption through Love" (to touch for once on the music), which at the end of *Götterdämmerung* rises from the burning of Valhalla, leads straight to the message of *Parsifal*.

BIBLIOGRAPHY

Writings by Wagner

Richard Wagners Sämtliche Schriften und Dichtungen, Volksausgabe, 16 vols., 6th edition, Leipzig, 1914. (All quotations from Wagner's texts, other than his letters, refer to this edition.)
Richard Wagner: *Skizzen und Entwürfe zur Ring-Dichtung* mit der Dichtung "Der junge Siegfried", ed. Otto Strobel, Munich, 1930.

Richard Wagner: *Sämtliche Briefe*, ed. G. Strobel and W. Wolf, 3 vols. to date, Leipzig, 1967–75.
Richard Wagner an Mathilde und Otto Wesendonk: Tagebuchblätter und Briefe, ed. Julius Kapp, Leipzig, 1915. (Ref. Wagner/Wesendonk).
Briefwechsel zwischen Wagner und Liszt, 2 vols., Leipzig, 1887. (Ref. Wagner/Liszt).
König Ludwig und Richard Wagner: Briefwechsel, ed. Otto Strobel, 5 vols., Karlsruhe, 1936–39. (Ref. Wagner/Ludwig).
Briefe an August Röckel von Richard Wagner, Leipzig, 1894. (Ref. Wagner/Röckel).
Richard Wagners Briefe an Theodor Uhlig, Wilhelm Fischer, Ferdinand Heine, Leipzig, 1888. (Ref. Wagner/Uhlig).
Richard Wagner: *Dramas*, trans. Ernest Newman, 5 vols., Leipzig, 1912.
Richard Wagner's Prose Works, trans. W. A. Ellis, London, 1892.
Richard Wagner: *My Life* (authorised translation), 2 vols., London, 1911.
Richard Wagner to Mathilde Wesendonck, trans. W. A. Ellis, London, 1905.
Correspondence of Wagner and Liszt, trans. F. Hueffer, 2 vols., London, 1888.
Richard Wagner's letters to August Röckel, trans. E. C. Sellar, Bristol, 1897.

Richard Wagner's Letters to his Dresden friends, Theodor Uhlig, Wilhelm Fischer, and Ferdinand Heine, trans. J. S. Shedlock, London, 1890.

Wagner's Sources

Bechstein, Ludwig: "Der Sängerkrieg auf Wartburg" in *Der Sagenschatz und die Sagenkreise des Thüringerlandes,* 4 vols., Hildburghausen, 1835–38.

Burnouf, Eugène: *Introducton à l'histoire de buddhisme indien,* Paris, 1844.

Burton, Sir Richard, trans.: "Women's Wiles" in Vol. 9 of *The Book of the Thousand Nights and a Night,* ed. Leonard C. Smithers, London, 1894.

Edda—Ettmüller, Ludwig, trans.: *Die Lieder der Edda von den Nibelungen,* Zurich, 1837.
    Grimm, the brothers: *Lieder der alten Edda,* Leipzig, 1815.
    Simrock, Karl, trans.: *Die Edda, die ältere und jüngere,* Stuttgart and Tübingen, 1851.

Fouqué, Friedrich Baron de la Motte: *Sigurd, der Schlangentödter,* Berlin, 1808.

Gottfrieds von Strassburg Werke, ed. F. H. von der Hagen, Breslau, 1823.

Tristan und Isolde von Gottfried von Strassburg, trans. Karl Simrock, Leipzig, 1855.

Gottfried von Strassburg: *Tristan,* trans. A. T. Hatto, Harmondsworth, 1960.

Gozzi, Carlo: *La donna serpente,* Venice, 1878 (published in Germany 1777–8).

Grimm, Jacob: *Deutsche Mythologie,* 2 vols., Göttingen, 1835.

Grimm, Wilhelm: *Die deutsche Heldensage,* Göttingen, 1829.

Heine, Heinrich: "Aus den Memoiren des Herrn von Schnabelewopski" and "Der Tannhäuser" in *Der Salon,* 4 vols., Hamburg, 1834–40.

Heinse, Johann J. W.: *Ardinghello und die glückseeligen Inseln,* Lemgo, 1787.

Hoffmann, E. T. A.: "Die Bergwerke zu Falun", "Der Kampf der Sänger" and "Meister Martin, der Küfner, und seine Gesellen" in *Die Serapions-Brüder,* 4 vols., Berlin, 1819–25.

Hoffmann, E. T. A.: *The Serapion Brethren,* trans. A. Ewing, 2 vols., London, 1886–92.

König, Heinrich: *Die hohe Braut,* Leipzig, 1844 (first edition 1833).

Lachmann, Karl: "Kritik der Sage von den Nibelungen" in *Zu den Nibelungen und zur Klage: Anmerkungen,* Berlin, 1836.

Laube, Heinrich: *Das junge Europa* (first edition 1833–37), *Gesammelte Schriften* vols. 7 and 8, Vienna, 1876.

Lohengrin—Görres, J., trans.: *Lohengrin, ein altteutsches Gedicht,* ed. F. Glökle, Heidelberg, 1813.

    Rückert, Heinrich, ed. *Lohengrin,* Quedlinburg and Leipzig, 1858.

Lytton, Edward George Earle Bulwer: *Rienzi, the Last of the Tribunes,* 3 vols., London, 1835.

Mone, F. J.: *Untersuchungen zur Geschichte der teutschen Heldensage,* Quedlinburg and Leipzig, 1836.

Müller, Wilhelm: *Versuch einer mythologischen Erklärung der Nibelungensage,* Berlin, 1841.

Nibelungenlied—Simrock, Karl: "Das Nibelungenlied" in *Das Heldenbuch,* vol. 2, Stuttgart and Tübingen, 1843.

    Hatto, A. T., trans.: *The Nibelungenlied,* Harmondsworth, 1965.

Sachs, Hans, *(Werke),* ed. J. A. Göz, Nuremberg, 1829.

Schopenhauer, Arthur: *Die Welt als Wille und Vorstellung,* Leipzig, 1819.

Schopenhauer, Arthur: *The world as Will and Idea,* trans. R. B. Haldane and J. Kemp, 3 vols., London, 1883.

Shakespeare, William: *Maass für Maass* in vol. 5 of *Shakspeares dramatische Werke,* trans. A. W. von Schlegel and L. Tieck, Berlin, 1831.

Simrock, Karl: *Wieland der Schmied,* Bonn, 1835.

Tieck, Johann Ludwig: "Der getreue Eckart und der Tannenhäuser" in *Phantasus*, 3 vols., Berlin, 1812–16.

Uhland, Ludwig: "Siegfrieds Schwert" (1812) in *Gedichte und Dramen*, 3 vols., Stuttgart, 1863.

Volsunga-Saga—Hagen, F. H. von der, trans.: "Volsunga-Saga" in *Nordische Heldenromane*, 5 vols., Breslau, 1814–28.

    Morris, William, trans.: *Volsunga Saga*, New York, 1962.

Wolfram von Eschenbach *(Werke)*, ed. Karl Lachmann, Berlin, 1833.

Wolfram von Eschenbach: *Parzival*, trans. Helen M. Mustard and Charles E. Passage, New York, 1961.

Books on Wagner

Adorno, Theodor W.: *Versuch über Wagner*, Frankfurt am Main, 1952.

Bertram, Johannes: *Mythos, Symbol, Idee in Richard Wagners Musikdramen*, Hamburg, 1956.

Dahlhaus, Carl: *Richard Wagners Musikdramen*, Velber, 1971.

Donington, Robert: *Wagner's 'Ring' and its Symbols*, London, 1963.

Drews, Arthur: *Der Ideengehalt von Richard Wagners dramatischen Dichtungen*, Leipzig, 1930.

Fries, Othmar: *Richard Wagner und die deutsche Romantik*, Zürich, 1952

Gál, Hans: *Richard Wagner: Versuch einer Würdigung*, Frankfurt am Main, 1963.

Golther, Wolfgang: *Richard Wagner als Dichter*, Berlin, 1904.

Gutman, Robert W.: *Richard Wagner. The man, his mind and his music*, London, 1968.

Mann, Thomas: "Leiden und Grösse Richard Wagners" and "Richard Wagner und der 'Ring des Nibelungen' "in vol. 9 of *Gesammelte Werke*, 12 vols., Frankfurt am Main, 1960.

Mann, Thomas: *Past Masters and other papers*, trans. H. T. Lowe-Porter, New York, 1942.

Mayer, Hans: *Richard Wagners geistige Entwicklung,* Düsseldorf and Hamburg, 1954.

Mayer, Hans: *Richard Wagner in Selbstzeugnissen und Bilddokumenten,* Reinbek bei Hamburg, 1959.

Newman, Ernest: *Wagner as Man and Artist,* London, 1914.

Newman, Ernest: *The Life of Richard Wagner,* 4 vols., London, 1933–47.

Raphael, Robert: *Richard Wagner,* New York, 1969.

Reich, Willi: *Richard Wagner: Leben-Fühlen-Schaffen,* Olten, 1948.

Shaw, George Bernard: *The Perfect Wagnerite,* London, 1898.

Westernhagen, Curt von: *Richard Wagner: sein Werk, sein Wesen, seine Welt,* Zürich, 1956.

Index

Achilleus 67
Adam, Adolphe 25
Aeschylus 67
Arabian Nights, The 24
Aristophanes 133
Art and Revolution 71, **72-73**
Auber, Daniel 11
Autobiographical Sketch 14, 15, 21, 31

Bakunin, Mikhail 66 note, 94
Battle of Parnassos, The 15
Bechstein, Ludwig 42
Beethoven, Ludwig van 7, 11, 16, 17, 74
Bellini, Vincenzo 20
Bergwerke zu Falun, Die **39-41**
Bianca und Giuseppe 41
Bismarck, Otto von 129, 132
Buddha 104, 105
Bulwer see Lytton
Burnouf, Eugène 104

Charlemagne 62
Chrétien de Troyes 141
Communication to my Friends, A 14, 28, 34, 53, 60, 64, 79, 80, 133
Death of Odysseus, The 15
Deinhardstein, Johann Ludwig 119
Dessauer, Josef 39
Devrient, Philipp Eduard 85
Dietsch, Pierre 36
Donington, Robert 80
Donizetti, Gaetano 11, 26
Edda 13, 81, 93, 102
Ettmüller, Ludwig 81 note
Euripides 67
Everyman 120

Fabre, Jules 133
Feen, Die 11, **18-20**, 23, 24
Feuerbach, Ludwig 66 note, 67, 75 note, 94
Fliegende Holländer, Der 11, **31-37**, 40, 43, 47, 48, 50, 51, 81, 97
Fouqué, Friedrich de la Motte 81 note
Franzosen vor Nizza, Die 42
Frederick II 38
Frederick Barbarossa 60, 61, 62, 63, 81
Friedrich Rotbart **61-62**

Gambetta, Leon Michel 133
German Opera, The 20
Geyer, Ludwig 15
Glückliche Bärenfamilie, Die **24-25**
Gluck, Christoph Willibald von 67
Goethe, Johann Wolfgang von 16, 17, 77, 119, 120, 125, 137
Golther, Wolfgang 81 note
Götterdämmerung 29, 63, 84, 85, 86, **93-96**, 100, 102, 132, 150
Gottfried von Strassburg 106, 108
Gounod, Charles 134
Gozzi, Carlo 18, 19, 34
Grass, Günther 120 note
Grimm, Jacob 81
Grimm, Wilhelm 81 note
Gutzkow, Karl Ferdinand 21

Hagen, F. H. von der 81 note
Hanslick, Eduard 116, 125
Heine, Heinrich 21, 31, 32, 43
Heinse, Johann 21

Hochzeit, Die 17, 18
Hoffmann, E. T. A. 16, 39, 40
  note, 43, 44, 46, 117
Hofmannsthal, Hugo von 19
  note, 40 note, 120 note
Hohe Braut, Die 26, 41
Hohenstaufen 38, 61, 62
Homer 15, 74
*How do republican aspirations
  stand in relation to monarchy?*
  61 note
Hugo, Victor 133, 134

Ibsen, Henrik 12, 137

Jesus 64, 67
Jesus von Nazareth **64-66**, 87,
  145
Joseph of Arimathea 136
Junge Siegfried, Der 26, 64, **87-
  92**

Kapitulation, Eine **132-134**
Kittle, Johann 42
König, Heinrich 26
Kosziuszko, Tadeusz 21

Lachmann, Karl 81 note
Laube, Heinrich 21
Leubald und Adelaide 16, 17
Liebesverbot, Das 11, 20, **21-24.**
  115
Liszt, Franz 87, 89, 90, 92, 105,
  106, 112
Lohengrin 9, 18, 19, 35, **53-59,**
  61 note, 63, 64, 67, 71, 81, 87,
  106, 115, 135, 136, 137, 142
Lortzing, Albert 7, 34, 120
Lucas, Professor 43
Ludwig II, King of Bavaria 14,
  23 note, 68, 147, 148
Luther, Martin 119 note
Luthers Hochzeit 119 note

Lytton, Bulwer 26, 34

Manfred, son of Frederick II 38
Männerlist grösser als Frauenlist
  24-25
Marschner, Heinrich 11, 17, 19,
  36
Meistersinger, Die 8, 12, 14, 46,
  52, 59,**115-131,** 132, 136, 137
Meyerbeer, Giacomo 11, 26, 29,
  36, 134
Mone, F. J. 81 note
Mozart, Wolfgang Amadeus 20,
  76
Müller, Wilhelm 81 note
'*Music Drama*', On the desig-
  nation 79
Music of the Future 78, 112
My Life 11, 14, 15, 31, 67, 94,
  115, 116 note, 135

Napoleon III 129
Nibelungenlied 74, 81
Nibelungen-Mythus, Der 63,**82-
  84,** 87
Nibelungen Saga 63
Nietzsche, Friedrich Wilhelm
  137
Novalis 114
Novize von Palermo, Die 21, 23

Offenbach, Jacques 133, 134
Ofterdingen, Heinrich von 43
Opera and Drama 7, 9, 71, **75-
  78,** 79, 90

Parsifal 8, 12, 14, 37, 46, 54, 66,
  69, 96, 105, 119 note, 132,
  135-150
Pillet, Léon 36, 41
Planer, Minna 23

Racine, Jean 76, 77

Raub des Rheingoldes, Der 90, 92
Reissiger, Karl Gottlich 41, 42
Religion and Art 148
Rheingold, Das 36, 84, 85, 89, **92**, 97, 144
Rienzi 11, **26–30**, 34, 39, 41, 61, 117
Ring des Nibelungen, Der 9, 14, 35, 36, 37, 52, 53, 55, 64, 66, 69, 70, 78, **80–103**, 104, 106, 107, 112, 132, 137
Röckel, August 95

Sachs, Hans 115, 116, 119, 120
Sarazenin, Die **38–39**
Schiller, Friedrich von 17, 77
Schopenhauer, Arthur 10, 94, 95, 103, 104, 106, 113, 114, 124, 148, 149
Schröder-Devrient, Wilhelmine 17, 20
Schumann, Robert 59 note
Scribe, Augustin Eugène 26, 41
Shakespeare, William 7, 11, 12, 15, 17, 21, 22, 23, 34, 55, 74, 76, 77, 137
Shaw, George Bernard 8, 80
Sieger, Die **104–105**
Siegfried 66, 84, 85, 94 note, **100–102**, 106, 112, 132
Siegfried Saga 77
Siegfrieds Tod 63, 64, 70, **84–94**
Simrock, Karl 81 note
Skizzen und Entwürfe zur Ring-Dichtung 89 note
Spontini, Gasparo 26, 29
Strobel, Otto 89 note

Tannhäuser 38

Tannhäuser 10, 35, 37, 39, 40, 41, **42–52**, 53, 54, 59, 63, 71, 78, 81, 106, 115, 133, 137
'*Tannhäuser*', On the staging of 48
Thomas, Ambroise 134
Tieck, Johann Ludwig 43, 44
Till Eulenspiegel 26
Tristan und Isolde 10, 35, 37, 52, 59, 96, 102, **104–114**, 115, 117, 135, 149

Uhland, Ludwig 81 note
Uhlig, Theodor 87, 133

Vaisseau fantôme, Le 36
Venusberg, Der 47
Verdi, Giuseppe 26
Volsunga Saga 81, 98

Wagner, Rosalie 17
Walküre, Die 84, 85, 89, 90, 92, **98–100**
Weber, Carl Maria von 11, 17, 19, 36
Weiss, Peter 120 note
Wesendonck, Mathilde 105, 106, 112, 114, 116, 136, 137, 148, 149
Wibelungen, Die **62–63**, 82
Wieland der Schmied **68–70**, 87
Wieland Saga 70, 75
Wittgenstein, Marie 112
Wolfram von Eschenbach 52, 53, 135, 136, 138 note, 141, 142, 144
Work of Art of the Future 70, 71, **73–75**